DREAMING OF A NEW AFRICA

QUESTIONS OR ANSWERS?

DREAMING OF A NEW AFRICA

QUESTIONS OR ANSWERS?

IRENEO OMOSITSON NAMBOKA

ISBN: 9789913981958

Cover Art and Typesetting by ArmUp Media

Printed and Bound in Uganda by Bonacraft Studios

Published by Ireneo Omositson Namboka with the services of
Scribe House,
P. O. Box 10722, Kampala, Uganda
www.scribehouse.ug
info@scribehouse.ug

To you, Stella Amoding and Clara Nafula,
my voiceless, deaf and blind daughter and
mother respectively; you opened my eyes to see life
as a daily privilege!

LIST OF TABLES

LIST OF FIGURES

ACKNOWLEDGEMENTS

This book is the result of so many kind people's intentional and inadvertent contributions, and so it would be impossible to mention all their names here. I wish to express my thanks to all of them. However, I owe much gratitude to my family, in particular to Robinah who bore the heavy burden of single-handedly caring for the children in every way and over so many years in my absence, away gathering the knowledge and human experience contained in this book.

Two friends to whom I am especially indebted are Professor Peter Mugyenyi, a life-long companion and soul mate whose thoughts, wisdom and convictions significantly influenced the message conveyed in this book. Samuel Musobya Kasamba, my other friend, played a vital role in spurring me forward both by asking me how far the manuscript had reached, discussing contents and ultimately identifying the publisher. Without these friends this work would not have seen the light of day.

I extend my gratitude to Scribe House Uganda, my publishers. I cannot thank Mrs Crystal Rutangye-Bazirake and all her team enough for their diligent, patient and tireless work that resulted in the production of this first of two books.

I express thanks to Ms Amina Dikedi, Ms Francesca Miller and Dr Oswald Ndolerire who generously offered their valuable time to review the manuscript. I owe the merits the reader will find reading this book to the people above, while any shortcomings should be attributed to my own human frailty.

Lastly, I thank Nicolas Francescetti, my Swiss comrade in the fight to return Africans to our original world greatness.

CONTENTS

INTRODUCTION

Years, decades and sometimes even an entire century can be lived – travelled through on this earth by an individual, without them leaving any trace behind.

Humans are endowed with a special, extraordinary, powerful tool – the brain – that puts their faculties of sight, hearing, expression and above all, that of cogitation, far above that of other known animate beings. But then this special capacity creates the need for accountability

After enjoying seven hundred and thirty two free safe moons in Africa, Europe, Asia and America, Koubaulou started to acutely feel a kind of debt. Most things around him looked unsatisfactory. He could not entirely blame the past generations for the status quo – after all, he did not exactly qualify to be called a member of the present generation – but with children of his own, aged between 24 and 38, Koubaulou certainly accepted the truth that he shared in the responsibility that the generation of his children placed on his generation, for the state that things were in. This was the point at which Koubaulou acknowledged the uselessness of a man who satisfied himself with only complaining over what was wrong, unfair or stupid about society in general, and particularly his own people – the Africans. Against the above, Koubaulou decided to write this book for posterity, as his personal witness, and to share his dream for Africa.

This book concerns six areas of the human condition, which the author covers in seven chapters. He looks at the situation within each theme, describes it as he sees it in context, and critically assesses the problems involved. He then raises questions which he invites the reader to think about, sometimes asking for an answer. The central message throughout the book is a complaint, sometimes presented as a warning, that individuals and groups in Africa lack rigour in their understanding and use of time. This flaw in lifestyle is inextricably tied to insufficient investment in critical thought and creativity.

'Dreaming of a New Africa' as a piece of writing, uses ideas that are original to start with because of the author's personal experience. These ideas are then combined with data obtained from reading, listening and imagination to produce interpretations that are submitted to the reader to digest.

The material in each part of the book had initially been prepared as independent papers that were presented at conferences attended by university students and academicians in the United States, several Non-Governmental Organizations on the defence of women's rights, as well as government and civil society representatives involved in the promotional awareness of the Universal Declaration of Human Rights. This makes it possible for one to either read the book from the beginning to the end or choose a given chapter, depending on one's particular interest.

The author stresses the urgency required for Africans to pause a little bit to interrogate their current lifestyle in order to ask themselves some critical questions about their 'innocence' on things that have not only affected the continent in the past but also the present and therefore risk hurting it even more tomorrow.

Many, if not most Africans today – whether on the continent itself or in the diaspora – live in unenviable conditions. Truthfully, some of these miserable conditions are centuries old, having afflicted some people well before the slave-hunting and trade eras that preceded colonization. However, the other part of the truth is that many of the shameful aspects of Africans' existence result from the unwillingness or incapacity of the continent's inhabitants to critically confront the crucial questions of survival. The capacity to do so may not have been sufficiently developed at the time of the earliest encounter between African ancestors and foreign invaders – probably thousands of years ago. This may have made the physical subjugation of unsuspecting and genuine Africans inevitable by unscrupulous crafty foreigners with military and political forces from the Middle East, Asia, and Western Europe.

The alien destroyers cleverly wrapped their agendas in attractive philanthropic smoke screens of morality, civilization and material advancement. For them, it was indeed their burden as white men to improve the deplorable and pitiable condition of primitiveness, backwardness and wretchedness in which African societies lived[1]. They reasoned that Africans had to be enslaved and later colonized to civilise and modernise them. Yet by the end of the Second World War in 1945, the generation of Africans such as Jomo Kenyatta, Cheikh Anta Diop, Kwame Nkrumah Abdel Gamal Nasser and Nelson Mandela, to name but a

---

1 There were the claims advanced to justify the systematic occupation of Africa based on the Berlin Conference convention of 1884-5. The original invasion of Africa, however dating back to over 5000 years ago was caused by Africa's attractiveness as an exceptionally wealthy, highly advanced and civilized place on earth. Read Chancellor Williams book *The Destruction of Black Civilisation – Great Issues of a Race from 4500 BC to 2000AD- 1974* – Third World Press.

few, were demanding an end to the masquerades and pretentiousness that alien rule in Africa was for the good of Africans. Independence, these brave men genuinely believed and asserted, was the hope for Africa.

Although very few African societies have been physically independent (in the modern sense of this word) for a hundred years, most have been so for at least half a century – if 1960 is considered the cut-off year between colonial occupation and independence[2]. Fifty years is not negligible time. The story of Singapore's political and economic experience in the same period shows this clearly. Why, then, has Africa's condition not changed for the better and instead, in most cases, actually deteriorated over the past half-century of self-rule or 'independence'?

Must Africans not engage in a genuinely intellectual, ethical and material self-examination about their lives now? Convinced that the answer to this question is in the affirmative is the reason I wrote this book. The European/Christian projects to civilise and modernise Africans have been severally and hotly debated. Whether or not the predominantly Western alien cultural influences in Africa were beneficial or destructive remains unsettled. As the title of this discussion presents the issue – considering the time lapse since the commencement of cultural intercourse between Africans and the West – albeit forced, can we now have a clear conclusion on whether the results of this interaction left Africans ruined or better off?

---

2 Over a century and a half ago, on July 26 1847, a country – perhaps the first nation on the continent to say no to foreign control – Liberia came into being. In 1885 at the Berlin Conference, Western colonial powers divided up Africa into today's states. A century later, Ghana, another West African nation on March 6, 1957, shook off the yoke of alien control. Guinea Conakry followed in 1958 only a year after.

This interrogation constitutes the heart of the discussion: Are the notions of 'Time' and 'Thought' critical in Africans' modes of existence? Isn't there a deficit if one compares present-day Africans with their ancestors on the one hand and other human societies present on the globe on the other? *"Atannayitaayita y'atenda nnyina okufumba"*[3] is an old African proverb that demonstrates this comparison.

The rest of this discussion freely borrows concepts from mainly oral African cultural wealth contained in spoken languages on the one hand, while on the other, it equally draws examples from technology as progressively lived in the West and in other parts of the world. Credit or blame to any given society at whatever historical period will be assigned to them as deserved.

---

3 Only a person who hasn't gone round places believes his mother's cooking is the best in the world.

TIME AND THOUGHT IN AFRICA

It has been falsely held in some respected Western milieu that Africans did not conceptualise time in their culture and daily life before colonisation. However, due to the different physical environments people grow up in, people's reflexes to time also differ; thus, when carefully looked at and well understood within their cultural intricacies, one will realise that all African societies fully punctuated their lives in terms of time. This chapter gives some examples of this.

D id the concept of 'time' exist in Africa before the Europeans' arrival?

One afternoon in the '90s, a friend of Koubaulou's, Mbath – a Senegalese engineer happily married to a French woman of Polish origin – were at the dining table. Mbath's English teacher, Koubaulou himself, had been invited to discuss general questions of interest. With the two families having developed close ties – Mbath's son and Koubaulou's daughter being agemates and living in the same residential area in the suburbs of Paris – these discussions were frequent. In the middle of the animated conversation, however, Mrs Mbath pointedly asked for Koubaulou's view on whether the notion of '*time*' existed in African cultures. Koubaulou was being asked this by a person of considerable literary enlightenment.

Mrs Mbath knew Koubaulou for being insistent on African things in general – a position she more or less respected him for. However, regarding this one issue, Koubaulou knew that his host truly wanted to push him to buy her view – one that most Europeans generally hold about Africans, namely that, traditionally, Africans had no notion of time.

It just happened that Koubaulou had been internally toying with this question for about five years already. He ventured to answer her that time as a concept did exist in his own culture and tradition. His friend's wife was very surprised. She thought Koubaulou was an 'objective' person who should have agreed with her view on this.

Koubaulou had the responsibility of not upsetting his gracious host but without forgetting to maintain his self-respect based on what he knew of his cultural upbringing. Gently, he explained the idea of the differences in perception that did not constitute factual differences.

Fortunately, this was a conversation among close friends. In a different setting, angry remarks would have been exchanged, as this would have been another occasion for the 'primitive Africans' to be told how time as a concept meant nothing to them, leading to the absence of any sense of the notion of 'planning' in their lives. Deep inside him, this very sentiment haunted Koubaulou.

Mrs Mbath loved literature and found African culture, particularly linguistics, a wealth of beauty. So turning to this field of her interest Koubaulou told her that if the notion of 'time' were to be non-existent in traditional African culture, the old sayings such as "*Akutwala ekiro omusiima bukedde*" or "*Akuyisa enkya omuyisa ggulo*"[4] would not exist either. The two families liked and trusted each other – a form of social capital Koubaulou enjoyed vis-à-vis Mrs Mbath that led her to seem to accept his standpoint on this sensitive subject. From that day, Koubaulou's thoughts have continued to expand on this fundamental commodity – *time*[5].

True, for most Africans on the continent like peasants, pastoralists, fishermen or hunters, who live in the natural environment, *time* may be a very different, abstract and imprecise concept. These people generally perceive time in broad terms like a year (season), a

4 "Gratitude towards he who forces you to get up early in the night to start the journey comes after the day heats up". or "He who overtakes you in the morning, you finally overtake him in the evening."

5 Nearly 5 years after starting to write on this theme the author had his position supported: *Negroes of Africa have and always have had their own ideas about the nature of the universe, time and space, about appearance and reality and about freedom and necessity.* (Carter Godwin Woodson, Annual Report of the Association for the Study of Negro Life and History, June 1933, The Mis-Education of the Negro, IAP 2010.)

moon (month), day or night. More precise may be the idea of sunrise, morning, noon, afternoon, sunset and evening. Even more precise notions of time are such moments labelled as 'cock-crow', 'dawn', or 'dewdrop evaporation' for the early part of the day, and then 'chickens return home', 'supper time', 'bed time', 'middle of the night' as well as 'white ants time' leading up to dawn refer to night time phases. Therefore, time consciousness is not less rigorous among bush dwellers as far as agreed moments or action plans are concerned. Actions related to travelling, catching fish, ants, or going to the garden before the hot sun sets all follow clear and well-elaborated notions of time.

This 'African' understanding of time is comparable to that of the Englishmen in Europe, for example, whose perception and expression of it through the image "*The early bird catches the worm*" is, interestingly, quite dissimilar from that of another European society – the French. Although so close to the English in many ways, and though they essentially have the same notion of time, the French express their concept of time using totally different images. In French the equivalent mental image is "*Le monde appartient à ceux qui se lèvent tôt*[6]." Is it not fascinating that, in essence, the first saying in Luganda, and both the English and French sayings are, indeed, saying one and the same thing?

Time as a concept cannot justly be said to be alien to African societies when in fact, just like societies in other parts of the world (here the comparison is with ancient European bush dwellers), the idea of seasons has always been real and continues to govern all human activities.

---

6 The equivalent to the English saying "The early bird catches the worm"

The above clarification should enable us to move from the immediate, that is to say, the 'daily' planning, to a longer-term organizational view of life's activities. African societies for centuries have been consciously engaged in procreation, animal husbandry, crop farming and predicting rains or droughts – thus developing highly developed cultures in which awareness of time before the arrival of foreigners from other continents happened. The question of how time was or is understood today in Africa by Africans becomes as interesting to investigate as are questions about African intellectual abilities, laziness, morals and ethics in general.

The Environment and Time Measurement Customs

Only a reductionist view of Africans' concept of time leads one to conclude that Africans did not have any notion of time. Those interested in looking at things closely, whether from Africa or industrialized societies, will easily appreciate the reasons why there may be differences in how the concept of 'time' varies from one environmental setting to another. Let's take an example of two children, say, aged seven years, but living in two different physical settings: we shall name the two children David and Kato. David is born in the suburbs of London in the borough of Hammersmith. Kato is born in Buyuki, a remote small village of Bulemeezi county about thirty miles away from Kampala in

Uganda. Each boy goes to the primary school nearest to their parents' home.

How is the environment going to impact the children's concept of time? We shall look at Kato's environment first. He wakes up with all his family at sunrise as the parents must start off early for the garden to avoid working in the hot sun. He walks to the main small village road, and there, he joins all the other children heading for school. They hear a distant gong from about three kilometres away – which signals they must hurry up now. Kato arrives with all the other children just in time to join the morning parade. Other children come in running and gasping for breath out of running most of the way. One must not arrive late, everyone knows. During the entire school day, time is strictly observed as bells are rung at the end of every lesson. Teachers often change with the end of lessons. Their break comes after the first three lessons, where everyone has a chance to go out and either play a little, go to the toilets or do anything preferred. A gong goes to mark the end of break time. Work in class resumes until the big lunch break is signalled by the bell when a hot meal is served.

Now, what about David's day? He wakes up with the chiming of the nearby church or cathedral clock. Moreover, he has always had a clock on the wall in his room, even before he was able to read or write. His father, who always wears a watch, offered David a *Swatch* watch on his sixth birthday. His mother too has a watch, and David must join his parents at breakfast at a quarter to seven in order to be able to run to the bus stop at twenty past seven, where the school bus collects the children from his location. The bus leaves the stage at exactly half-past seven, and therefore he has to be there in time. There is only one bus which he cannot afford to miss. Should he miss it, he will be in big trouble with both the school and his parents. Before the bus leaves, there is a roll call to ensure all the children are on board or to know who is not. There is a large clock on the bus which all children can see, all the time.

The school entrance gate closes once all the children from the bus have entered. Every pupil has a copy of the day's and weekly timetable with every lesson clearly shown and time indicated against it plus the name of the teacher responsible. David frequently checks the time from the watch he wears on his wrist and anticipates every coming item on the timetable. When he starts to feel hungry, he looks at the watch and knows for how much longer he still has to wait – not long or, oh dear, another half hour to go!!!!

The differences in the notions of time that these two children have should easily be seen here. David is surrounded by tools, processes, and actions which make him constantly and minutiously track '*time*'. It is almost impossible for him to spend ten minutes without time being part of his thought process. On the other hand, Kato lives in an environment where this 'second to second' and 'minute to minute' time-tracking is absent. There are neither church bells nor wristwatches for him. There was neither breakfast time to respect nor a school bus to catch. He is perfectly aware of time, but his reflexes in adherence to it are different.

Most mature and serious Africans will have grown up in a different technological environment setting from that where Westerners grew up. This clearly shows why the former may exhibit less restlessness about time in situations where the latter are literally panicking. This is not because Africans do not have an equivalent concept of time. It is the environmental conditioning that brings in the differences. It is, in fact, a confession of cultural ignorance on the part of those who rush to such reductionist conclusions about the absence of the time notion among African societies.

The term *restlessness* has been deliberately used above, although others could have opted for *impatience* instead. The important point here is to establish that Africans, like other human societies, operate fully aware of the "time" dimension in life. It is on the very basis of this fact that we now set out to ironically challenge most of Africa's elite who seem to be oblivious about time.

II

TIME IN RELATION TO PERFORMANCE AND PROGRESS

Now that the notion of time as a concept in traditional African cultures is addressed, we must turn to the troubling issue of its relevance in relation to problem-solving in Africa. For instance, is it not legitimate to ask what work has been accomplished by succeeding generations in Africa over the last half-century, ever since their independence from the colonialists?

This chapter illustrates the 'performance' and 'progress' concepts in modern or post-colonial Africa. However, since Africa's performance and progress follow Western models, examples of brain work from the West have been contrasted in this chapter with one from Africa.

The reader will progressively see that even though the notion of time isn't alien to African societies, the level of technological advancement to overcome natural limits to man's abilities over the centuries in the West have outperformed Africans' advancements by far. Achievements in medicine, space and IT are clear examples of this. The chapter thus attempts to draw Africans' attention to the often concealed wrong beliefs they hold about Africa. One such wrong idea is that Africa is naturally a poor continent and that expecting aid from the West is natural and must continue. Another self-demeaning belief is that dependency on inventions from Europe is a predestined condition. This chapter openly denounces any African who believes in such fallacies, whoever he/she may be. The chapter calls upon Africans to take stock of what has been achieved over the seventy years since alien rule was eliminated from the continent. It laments the absence of intellectual rigour, lack of new original initiatives in solving societal problems and the perpetual imitation of Western models of doing things that have largely failed to work locally.

In African customs, it used to be common practice that a little child of a village dweller, as early as his seventh year of age, went with his parents to the field with an appropriate implement such as a miniature hoe appropriate to his size. As work progressed, people turned back to see how much ground they had covered so far from time to time. This is how in the end, the family decided whether it had done a reasonable job before they could leave the field to go back home satisfied. This is a very simple but typical African image that anyone familiar with peasant life understands.

Critically looking at undertakings by Africans today, the impression one gets is that this instinctive inclination by ordinary Africans to constantly assess performance while carrying out a task is now prominently lacking, if not simply absent. African leaders responsible for running countries, ministries or state-owned institutions have a hard job to prove otherwise. It is not a secret that some villagers have been heard to utter such unsettling statements as "things were better under foreign colonial rule." Sadly, indeed looking around in many places today on the African continent, fifty years of independence has seen the deterioration and sometimes real disappearance of once enviable infrastructures such as roads, rail trucks, hospitals, police barracks, cotton research institutions, schools and many social service systems. Time as a factor has meant diminution instead of expansion or improvement in most areas. Does time count, then, in Africans' existence?

It would be a serious and uninformed insult to suggest that societies such as the Pygmies of the Ituri Forest, the Khoesan of the Kalahari Desert, the Maasai of the Nyika Plateau and the Amboseli plains in Kenya or the Karamojong of North-eastern Uganda have no sense of time and that time means nothing to them. All these societies have had considerably minimal direct interaction with the western forms of civilization; they largely still live a mode of life their grandparents lived fifty years ago or more. But are they not constantly integrating the time factor in their lives and in their daily activities? One aspect of life which they all share is ensuring their existence. This is all time-based: A family originally consists of a woman and a man. Immediately the two are united in marriage, the eyes of society are fixed on them with the expectation that within a given (approximate) lapse of time, a child will be born. Tracking is performed by the parents and the expanded family. The woman's body form is watched while more intimate relatives such as the aunt, sister, mother and others will inquire about the status of the menstrual cycles. The community at large will start to be anxious if several moons or seasons go by without the wife showing any signs of being pregnant. Is time not central in all this?

When a child is born, whether it is a girl or boy, measuring time becomes even more important. There are ceremonies: naming, extracting teeth, circumcision, initiation into womanhood or manhood, etc. Time is constantly a central element. Marriage finally comes as a time marker, and the individuals recommence the cycle.

Independent of human life, Africans traditionally reasoned with time as a crucial parameter. Herders of cattle, sheep, camels or goats, and those who raise poultry look at units with time in mind as the factor of multiplication. Acquisition of a cow comes with an ambition that, over time, the cow will produce a calf or even two where luck is high. They knew that over time from one cow, there would be a herd. Indeed in two Ugandan languages, the word herd happens also to mean a hundred.[7] Most societies in Eastern Uganda practiced the tradition of offering small chickens to a child who visited his uncle or aunt for the first time. The whole message that this gift symbolized was that both the child and the chick would grow into mature beings with time. The chick will sooner than later become a hen or cock. Whichever is the case, there is jubilation with seeing the little bird develop into a big rooster or a hen, which in turn lays eggs and produces many little other ones. Time, hope increase, and improvements are the norm in the traditional African psych.

Modern Africans have largely adopted the western ways of viewing life – viewing ourselves with regard to material property we aspire to own. Africans who have retained the traditional yardstick for measuring developments in individual and collective matters criticize what seems to be sheer blind noisy talk and activism on the part of those holding public offices who appear not to realize that for half a century now, development, where it has not been regressing, has in fact been nil. This may sound like an outrageous charge if taken purely as a matter of politicking.

Concretely, statistics on country performance in Africa concerning a few crucial fields over the past years since independence graphically illustrate this absurdity. For example, the tourism industry is one of the biggest foreign currency earning assets that many African

7 Igana in Runyankole means a hundred and Eggana in Luganda means very many cows.

countries such as Uganda, the Democratic Republic of the Congo, Rwanda and Burundi could optimally exploit. However, this is very far from being the case. Fichaka Fayissa et al.'s August 2007 study attributed only 5% of the total world figure of 444 million tourists – i.e. 37 million, to Africa[8]. In the case of Uganda, tourism ranked as the third most important foreign exchange earner at the time of independence in 1962, with the wild game as a leading attraction to visitors. Although ranked the world's 10th in possessing the most diversified range of mammalian species, Uganda has not been able to protect its animal population over time[9].

The question is still to be answered as to whether modern or westernized Africans relate <u>time</u> with <u>thought in what they do</u>. Primitive societies did, and villagers who are less impacted by modernity still cling to rigorous optimization in using their days and nights even if they do not measure time in seconds, minutes or hours. We have illustrated this in regard to African bush dwellers. It is now time to illustrate the absurdity of how modern Africans use time.

Time and Thought

Very early, as soon as children start school – hardly after primary school, a girl or boy will have learnt how to tell time from a clock or a wrist watch. The notion of a year – meaning twelve months, fifty-two weeks or three hundred and sixty-five days and even the particular

8 http://www.mtsu.edu/economics/FacPapers/TourismAfricawp.pdf
9 In Environment and Natural Resources Series – Enhancing Wildlife's Contribution to Growth, Employment and Prosperity, pp4 (followed by pp11)

case of the "leap year" depending on the length of the second month of the year are well grasped. Africans will learn all this by heart and live with it throughout life without ever turning around to ask questions about the significance of measuring time this way. Perhaps this is where the fault lies in the education people receive.

But why is this so? It is because 'thinking' or rather 'critical thinking' is hardly ever touched on or encouraged. Education or studying is all about cramming facts as listed above – like a parrot memorizes what it hears. If people in Africa made just a little effort to think about the learned facts about life, perhaps things in life would assume a different reality.

Let us consider luck. The idea of being unlucky or lucky or endowed with natural resources or not, for instance, needs to be placed in the context of 'time'. It is the received belief among people abroad and in Africa today that Africans are poor, and so is the African continent: not rich – i.e. not endowed with the riches which the developed countries of Europe and America, Japan or now, China, have. This operating mentality makes people in Africa accept that they are unlucky and poor - in comparison to Europeans, and therefore expect, as a right, that economic aid must be given to them. Is truth not eluding the African while the European, in his sense of humour, leaves the theatrical drama to continue? "*Mujinga anawumia*" goes a Kiswahili saying and "*Omujega afa alaba*" the Baganda jest. Time and thought in Africa?

It was the European, of course, who went with the habit of going about life by minutely measuring time from the broad notions of time which that the Africans shared with him in terms of seasons, moons, days and nights into tiny units called hours, minutes and seconds with the calendar, clock or wrist watch as tools. Africans learned perfectly well the use of the tools but stopped there. What was not done was trying to find out about this time measuring business – that is, the application of seconds, minutes, hours, days, weeks, months to the wider life control with which nature confronts us. Shallow thinking is the killer.

The Misnomer of Africa being a Poor Continent!

In the logic of natural endowments, there is no justification for the claim that Africans have less than Europeans, as far as time is concerned. The British do have a saying which clearly states that *"time is money"*. But like Europeans, Africans have equal quantities of time from nature – or must this basic geographical fact be explained to the African reading this page? If this is so, why do the latter end up having less money and having to turn to the former for budget support, capital for investment and aid? The explanation is hidden in how Africans (mis)understand time and (mis)use it. This brings us to the second part of this section's title – *thought*.

Let us haphazardly take two countries – one from Europe - Sweden and another from Africa Kenya – and talk comparatively. In a year, there are only twelve months – for the Kenyans and the Swedes. This is the same as saying 365 days for both peoples in the year. Is this not an indisputable fact? But the African turns to the European, asking, or actually, begging for financial aid. Draught or famine may be claimed to justify African countries' begging habit. Europeans sometimes feel obliged to subject their positive response to Africans' self-ridiculing appeals to some conditions. Some European citizens at home, away from the diplomatic front known to most African people, scream against dishing money out to people abroad they deem lazy and irresponsible, while at home in Europe they face serious difficulties in their daily lives. Do many Africans know about this anger in the "rich" European nations? Maybe these ordinary people in Europe have a point, which African children in schools and many men in leadership positions should learn about.

Why and how can an African possibly be writing about this? This is the kind of question that thousands of people suffering from starvation, disease and wars in Africa would ask in disbelief. This would easily be perceived as support to Europe's refusal to give away money to help Africa. 'Who is bad?' went the late Michael Jackson's song! It is the enfeebled thinking faculties of the beggar from Africa which is bad. In the final analysis, it is the African who is bad by reducing himself to that status. Otherwise, objectively, the truth is that it is not the African who should be going around begging or expecting aid from the European fellow dweller on the earth's surface. Explaining the absurdity involved here requires only an elementary understanding of arithmetic and geography that any secondary school pupil in Africa possesses. Below is the explanation, if it must be given:

If, as stated above, there are twelve months in the year, which are then broken down into seasons in Europe and in Africa, there is no inequality. If, however, anyone should complain about inequality based on seasons, it should be the Europeans who are seriously disadvantaged - for the following reasons. While in a country such as Kenya, people can freely graze in open natural pastures all year round, this is not possible for pastoralists in Sweden, Switzerland, Norway, or Great Britain. *Why?* a young African pupil in school might logically ask. Below is the answer:

Instead of the twelve months of natural sunshine punctuated by occasional down pours of welcome rainy seasons enjoyed by farmers in Africa, in Europe only six out of the twelve months have such climatic conditions when the weather is described to be enjoyed by farmers' animals and crops. The other part of the year – from about late October to early May – at least six of the months in the year, temperatures outside are drastically low. Autumn – from the end of September, temperatures steadily drop, reaching freezing point from December. This makes any form of outdoor life for plants and animals impossible until around the end of February, when spring starts. This is comparable to bush fires raging in Africa for an equivalent period of time – leaving all plants and animals without life! In winter, therefore, life literally comes to a stop. People must find alternative solutions to survive, including creating artificial shelters to keep animals warm and fed. Equipment must be created for artificial lighting and watering to last people and their animals in the harsh winter conditions. The severity of nature under the winter conditions -a yearly challenge can only be fully appreciated by those who live in Europe. Quite often, several lives are lost where the elderly, disabled, drunkards, homeless or very poor cannot provide sufficiently for themselves. In these countries, hard work is the key to survival. This presupposes really hard thinking about survival. If an African survives thirty winters and fails to wake up to these cruel realities, conclude: he is a nincompoop.

Therefore, it is against the odds of the less favourable time and natural resources to live on that the inhabitants in Europe manage to stay alive. It is with these enormous yearly climatic challenges that Europeans see the inhabitants from paradise zones on earth's surface – Africa – turning up, hat in hand to beg for aid! With no shame, Africans find themselves and their nation's poor begging for, or at best, seeking to import items such as powder milk and tinned beef from Europeans. This must sometimes amuse inhabitants of European countries. The drama on the stage is, in reality, pathetic, ridiculous and regrettable. Is this too due to colonialism? What do Africans have to show for the fifty years of independence if this continues?

It is not given to everyone to see what is obvious – at least not at the same speed. For this reason, even when everything was to be distributed with almost perfect equality among people, the end result of utilizing them would vary considerably. Take the example of students in a classroom. Think about a simple situation where there are, say, thirty pupils in the final year of primary school. A teacher, the same person, stands before the class and teaches a lesson – say in geography. Before the end, he asks the students to answer ten simple questions given in the relevant textbook. He collects the students' exercise books which he marks, and the following day, he makes the marks obtained by each student known to the class.

It is not unusual to find that scores range from very high to incredibly low ones. If the teacher marked out of, say 20, the scores might vary from as high as 20/20; 19/29; 18/20, gradually decreasing until the lowest could be 7/20! The girl or boy who gets the best mark in the class may not be the teacher's favourite, just as the last one could be the pupil the teacher likes most.

Like other societies or nations, Africans are in a global classroom where the Creator is the teacher. The sun shines for everyone every day. When rain falls, it wets everywhere and helps the crops of anyone who cared to sow in time. Apart from equally distributing means to all humans, nature will not interfere with how individuals live their lives. Over two thousand years ago, a Great teacher gave a parable of three servants who were each entrusted with two talents by the same master before he went away on a journey. On returning, the servants were called to bring to the master what had been entrusted to each of them. The reader should choose which of the three servants resembles the Africans' situation most.

The thoughts conveyed through the above images – first, Uganda's wild game, which is dwindling but had been the country's fabulous tourist attraction once upon a time. Second, Africans' genuine belief in their inherent poverty, being less favoured by nature while at the same time regarding Europeans as more affluent and that these must therefore assist Africans overcome poverty. Finally, the unequal performance levels by students who have the same teacher, textbooks, and the same amount of time to answer set questions lead us to return to the vexing question: Are Africans putting time and thought to use at all?

What if Africans' calamity, both individually and collectively, largely stemmed from abandoning the old habits of focusing on a problem, concentrating all thought and time on it until a solution is arrived at? What if the African genius practically withers out of existence by allowing others to force external solutions to strictly local problems? This brings to mind a light-hearted remark made by Thabo Mbeki in 2004 at the Africa regional preparatory conference on the Convention concerning the Rights of Persons with Disabilities. The then President of South Africa warned that there were aid givers out there with large sums of money to dish out who, however, gave the recipient both the money he needed together with the list of problems which the recipient must address and on which to spend it. Koubaulou was present in the conference room and made a note of the anecdote. Later on, the participants, who were mainly persons with disabilities, would feel encouraged to reiterate their slogan of "Nothing for us without us". A few months later, the CARS would be launched in Pretoria. This acronym had nothing to do with vehicles! The 'CARS' stood for **C**entre for **A**frica's **R**enaissance **S**tudies. The French term "*renaissance*" has conveniently become an English word with specific reference to that cut-off point in the Middle Ages when in Europe, the Enlightenment brought an end to earlier ancient beliefs, many of which would not stand the simplest test of scientific questioning. In daily use, the word *naissance* as it appears in passports under the rubric "*Date de naissance*" simply means birth as in 'Date of *birth*'. 'CARS', therefore, is about the rebirth of Africanness. It must be out of profound concern on the part of the founders of CARS that Africans need a truly rude shake-up to be reawakened. A mental shock may be.

For over fifty years as independent countries, African peoples have been dutifully applying philosophies, using implements and following models of thought provided or sometimes even imposed from foreign 'advanced' societies. The balance sheet shows a negative end. Out of frustration, blame has been hurled at those who have been partners to 'develop' Africa. The painful and yet only secret to solving Africa's perennial unsolved problems is to revisit the issues of "time" and "thought". Elsewhere this appears to have been the cure.

Outside Africa, modern management methods underline the importance of time measurement in evaluating performance, productivity, efficacy and efficiency. The field of exact sciences provides staggering illustrations of improvement in results, quality of products and overall progress, which come with time. Africans must become curious and take an interest in what has been done elsewhere. Specifically, this entails attentively directing their minds to this 'time dimension' within endeavours aimed towards progress. A few concrete examples will help to show this clearly. First, let us take the invention of the first automated aircraft by the Wright brothers about a century ago, in 1903. The vaunted aircraft in question was not even capable of sustaining itself up in the air for a single complete minute! The fact is that the history making flight only lasted 59 seconds in the air before the craft fell to the ground (not landed)! It only covered a total distance of hardly ¼ of a kilometre (852 feet exactly) on the ground. Nevertheless, man had flown for the first time, and the entire world celebrated that "history-making" flight. Yes, at that time, a hundred years ago, the event was breath-taking.

The clumsy gadget in question could have been rightly described as having been laughable in very many ways today. It carried no passenger as there was no extra seat; there was no toilet facility on it, no reading light, no air conditioning or an oxygen mask as an emergency precaution. Even more dangerous to imagine, although the aircraft successfully took off, it never landed but "in one of its darts downward, struck the ground"[10]. The rest of its features would not impress a reader who is only familiar with the aircrafts as we know them today. Take the speed at which it flew, for instance. Given that the distance covered was 852 feet in less than one minute, it remained suspended in the air. It follows that the aircraft flew at a speed of 9.7 mph - (15½ km/hour).

Yet in less than a hundred years - by the end of the 1990s, engineers in aviation had made stunning improvements to aircrafts. The French and British aviators were able to produce the aeroplane they called the 'Concord' with the capacity of 1,614 mph (cruising speed) that enabled it to cross the Atlantic Ocean flying from London to New York in just three hours! In terms of the capacity of aircrafts to sustain themselves in the air against their weight, the Jumbo 747 was comfortably staying seven hours in the air to perform

---

10 See Wikipedia Wright brothers -From Wikipedia, the free encyclopedia (http://en.wikipedia.org/wiki/Wright_brothers) Wilbur started the fourth and last flight at just about 12 o'clock. The first few hundred feet were up and down, as before, but by the time three hundred ft had been covered, the machine was under much better control. The course for the next four or five hundred feet had but little undulation. However, when out about eight hundred feet the machine began pitching again, and, in one of its darts downward, struck the ground. The distance over the ground was measured to be 852 feet; the time of the flight was 59 seconds. The frame supporting the front rudder was badly broken, but the main part of the machine was not injured at all. We estimated that the machine could be put in condition for flight again in about a day or two. (Consulted on May 19,2013.)

the same journey. Imagine and compare the difference in the weight of the aircraft the Wright brothers flew for less than a minute and that of the Jumbo 747 that remains afloat for seven hours. Everyone knows that aircrafts today can take off, land comfortably, and sustain themselves for practically as long as necessary with several features to give safety, entertainment, and comfort. Such has been the extent of improvement or progress over time in terms of the quality and performance of the aircraft as a product in aviation.

Astronomy and the performance of astronauts and satellites today could easily be said to belong to the domain of the supernatural.

Scientific work also shows incredible progress over time in another domain of human endeavour – for instance, the automobile industry. Arguments may abound about who invented the first automobile or car, but Nicolas Joseph Cugnot, a Frenchman, is credited for inventing the first self-propelled road vehicle in 1769. Few people know what the features of that first vehicle were. The machine that mesmerized witnesses at the time of its invention could only run at a speed of four kilometres an hour or (2½ mph). It carried no passengers. It had to stop every ten to fifteen minutes to build up steam power. The following year the inventor produced a vehicle that could carry four passengers. If one concentrates on just one aspect of this product, namely the engine, the improvement made upon it over time must strike any observer. About one hundred years after Cugnot's above engine model, a German engineer, Karl Benz, turned up a vehicle powered by a four-stroke cycle gasoline engine in 1885. In comparison to the 1769 gadget, the car became commercially sold in 1888 with a ¾ horsepower capacity to do 13kms (8miles) per hour.

By 2008, 120 years from the release of the first commercialized car, the product "vehicle" had phenomenally metamorphosed into a bullet-like item: 480 horsepower, capable of reaching the speed of 60 mph in less than four seconds and topping out at 193 mph. Similar enquiries in other scientific fields such as of medicine, physics, astronomy, or informatics will bring out equally mind-boggling examples.

African thought must be stirred up and energized by the forgoing information on the relationship between time and brainwork. Considering what is essential – it may be critical to reconsider what has been learned as being the most important natural resource man is endowed with. What if it was **time** and the **human mind**?

On the whole, African societies viewed as new nations have had a relatively short span of time over which to demonstrate that with passing time, investment in thought and action are increasingly changing for the better. With its independence dating back to 1847, Liberia could be Africa's first independent country on the continent- predating the generally known African states, societies or nations within the international community. It becomes legitimate then to expect that with over a century and a half of existence, exercising self-rule and pursuing the objectives of development, time has been used as a beneficial factor to transform the living conditions of the Liberian people and the evolutionary trend of the state. Of course, other relatively old independent societies or countries such as Ethiopia, Ghana, Egypt, Guinea Conakry, and the

DRC (Congo Kinshasa) inspired this discussion. This was because they have all been running their own affairs as sovereign states for at least half a century. Discussing this 'Africans' problem would be incomplete without bearing in mind the continent's dispersed descendants living in the Diaspora. This is where the republic of Haiti with its independence dating as far back as 1803 must be mentioned. The discussion can now turn to the question of how the parameters of time and thought have played out in the course of human performance for African peoples over the years.

Africans invented independence struggles, self-rule and government institutions as far back in history as Pharaonic times or even before. What is true also, however, is that in this domain of human endeavour, African societies, once the new nations mainly resulting from European colonial powers' partitioning of the continent in 1885 into what constitutes African states, gained independence - slightly over six decades or so ago -after intense interactions with the Western world, they largely abandoned the old forms of organizing life in common as nations. Once self-governing, they each adopted elaborate programmes containing ambitious objectives for the future. This field involved practical and concrete planned actions - typically, countries express these in the form of National five-year Development Plans. Constitutions and laws based on Western models existed in almost every African state to provide the normative frameworks where the plans were executed. Questions have to be asked as to what is the performance of these new entities like? Haiti in the Caribbean and Liberia on the Africa continent are the oldest. Their political and economic histories are well documented today – and the names President Duvalier (Papa Doc) and President Charles Taylor are perhaps 'notoriously' known to everyone. For this discussion, however, these two cases of close to "failed States" will not be dealt with in detail here for two main considerations. First, in large part the 'Africans' who did run these countries from independence for nearly a hundred years were descendants of African slaves whose real cultural, and therefore, mental Africanness may have been considerably affected by extraneous factors. The extent to which merits or flaws in the systems they put in place to run their countries may be attributed to Africa or Western societies where they evolved cannot be easily decided.

Societies with truly indigenous leaders are a preferable option to consider here. Uganda, because of its unique history and geographical location astride the equator – thus belonging both to the continent's north and south presents interesting characteristics to be looked at although, in common with most other 'new' African states created by the arbitrary drawing of borders that marked out colonial entities as the property of one or other of the European powers at the Berlin Conference in 1885, Uganda has the following features:

> • Its arbitrary borders went through the middle of many existing African small nations to the north, East and West and South West except to the south where the great Lake Nalubaale (later to be named after the British queen at the time the first Europeans saw it (Queen Victoria).
> • Inside the borders are enclosed some thirty distinct language and cultural human groups

which considered themselves to be nations but were labelled 'tribes' by the colonial ethnologists and anthropologists to distinguish them from 'nations' - a term reserved only for civilized societies in Europe.

• The establishment of the colonial presence was accompanied by the introduction of subjects of the British old empires (India in this case) who belonged to a race other than that of the rulers themselves.

• The language of the colonizing power, although spoken by a very tiny minority in the country at the time of independence, was made the official/ national language.

• Granting of independence was predicated on the semblance that Ugandans could run their country on exactly the British bicameral Parliamentary system of government.

• Historical disputes in which Britain was centrally involved but to which a solution hadn't been found before independence was left to Ugandans themselves to sort out.

• Some traces of distant religious rivalry in which the colonial power had been involved resulted in a kind of proxy wars between Ugandans - with Protestants and Catholics, on the one hand, grimacing at each other while on the other hand Christians, in general, looked at Muslims suspiciously[11].

---

11   from   http://en.wikipedia.org/wiki/Ugandan_general_election,_1962
- "However, new elections were held in April 1962, and Kiwanuka's party lost to an alliance of Milton Obote's Uganda People's Congress and the Buganda traditionalist party, Kabaka Yekka, with **Kiwanuka's Catholicism making him unpopular with his fellow Buganda**, a mainly Protestant people. (Emphasis author's) See also Yoga Adhola in UPC and the Elections of 1961 and 1962 - The two forces and the antagonism between them had been forged in the religious conflicts

How has this mixed bag of cultures fared through the fifty years since the attainment of independence? How does the "Time and thought" discussion bring out what transpired and how does the future of a country like this look? This takes us back to the phenomenal progress made by people engaged in the domain of exact sciences over the last century. Not that one expects similarly spectacular leaps in the case of Uganda, but some concrete advancement is fair to expect.

Outside Uganda, Africans have demonstrably deployed efforts to produce results in literature or authorship. In this, the endeavours are usually mainly directed to political, cultural and related socio-economic issues of concern to citizens. Thinkers such as Cheikh Anta Diop, Chinua Achebe, Ali Mazrui, Wole Soyinka, Amadou Ampaté Bah and Joseph Ki Zerbo, to name but a few, have thoroughly applied their intellectual talents for practically their entire lives. Bearing in mind the collective efforts by these personalities this discussion attempts to establish whether, with the passing time over the last fifty years, there was a qualitative incremental trend in the products they brought forward to the world, particularly to Africa's needs.

This field of mostly abstract African intellectual craftsmanship differs considerably from the mainly physical one reviewed earlier. It also clearly differs from the spectacular performance record shown by Africans in the domain of sports and games on the world stage.

and wars that characterized Buganda in the last quarter of the 19th century. The antagonism between the two forces reached its peak when in February 1892 they fought a pitched battle as Protestants and Catholics, and the Protestants assisted by Captain Lugard won the war. Subsequent to this victory a Protestant oligarchy was established in Buganda, and Catholics were discriminated against in the appointment of chiefs. This state of affairs obtained throughout the entire colonial period, and eventually constituted the grievance upon which the DP was based. Formed in 1954, the DP was essentially organized to redress the discrimination of Catholics.(http://www.upcparty.net/history/election_61and62.htm)

Africans have persistently outperformed other peoples in this latter domain even though, ironically, the key measurement criterion of excellence here is even more critically "time".

We will concentrate here on an individual or a group of persons engaging in an intense and sustained mental effort that may stretch over time to produce an entirely new item or product. In cases where the new product is of the same kind as others before it, the examination will consist of comparing the latest one with older ones to bring out what could be described as 'added value' or improvement on the earlier products of the same kind. The newer item should be accorded higher points to the extent that it elevates the intrinsic quality or value. In literature or in governance, it is about the extent to which a literary product or policy innovation shows itself to be betterment on earlier ones for society. Within the context of this reflection, we should start at the African continental level by looking at the literary domain's most outstanding endeavours over the past half-century or so. At the country level, Uganda's experience in establishing a positive (upward) or negative (downward) trend by the successive leaders from 1962 to the present will also be objectively evaluated. Cross-references will be made using available data on other countries in the world as well.

World Intellectual Productivity, Recognition and their Relevance to Africa.

The 1986 Nobel Prize laureate for literature was an African Professor– the celebrated Nigerian Wole

Soyinka, Africa's first in the field. Most literary Africans, particularly those in academia from countries of the Commonwealth, saw this African playwright as having been "raised" to the calibre of earlier luminaries and noble minds such as William Shakespeare, who had lived and written nearly four centuries before him. With this, following the logic guiding this discussion, the mind returns to the achievements which were earlier listed in the field of pure sciences – aviation and the automobile industries. It was demonstrated that each subsequent product within the same category significantly improved on earlier ones. In this regard, it becomes necessary for the literary world to evaluate the inherent literary or philosophical *added value* in work that Professor Wole Soyinka produced to merit the Nobel Prize against those which a world-renowned playwright and author, William Shakespeare, produced roughly three and a half centuries earlier.

This approach is adopted here in view of the fact that the world today is grappling with issues of man's failure to live peacefully with one another due to ideological, religious, racial or simply cultural intolerance; while brotherhood and mutual trust continue to elude even human societies that are essentially of the same stock, and in particular because, sadly, an independent African country Rwanda ended up sinking into immeasurable shame with the 1994 horrendous killings estimated to have reached a million fellow citizens. The root of all that human folly was intolerance.

However, discrimination, intolerance and the rejection of the other plus other forms of bestialities aren't new among humans. In fact, this comes out very clearly in two of Shakespeare's works. The contents of his plays, "The Merchant of Venice" and "Othello", strikingly bring out this point. Therefore, in this comparative discussion, the two great literally minds shall be evaluated by comparing how each of them handled these challenges to humanity in the context of each writer's epoch. To what extend can the messages contained in the works of the world's 1986 greatest author be said to be an improvement on those which the greatest English literary man of the seventeenth century[12] whom the English-speaking world has acclaimed as an unequalled world literary brain?

Two very famous literary pieces of work by William Shakespeare, produced for the entertainment of the people of his time, are looked at in the following paragraphs. On close scrutiny, it comes out that Shakespeare entertained by demonizing some human groups and in that way, probably inadvertently sowing seeds of hate and rejection directed at some minority groups in Europe. Take the caricature of the Jew he makes with the character of Shylock in The Merchant of Venice. There is also an insidious element of revenge to which the spectators are entertained, although this is precisely what the Jew in the play is being told not to seek. What surrounds the fate of Shylock speaks tons on anti-Semitism. That was a long time ago, in 1596.

12 The dates given when William Shakespeare wrote the two plays considered here are 1596 for the Merchant of Venice and 1604 for Othello. – (Source: http://absoluteshakespeare.com/trivia/timeline/timeline.htm) - Shakespeare Timeline describes the many chapters in Shakespeare's colourful life. From humble beginnings in Stratford to his marriage to the older Anne Hathaway and popular acclaim for his works, Shakespeare Timeline follows the life of literature's most famous playwright.

A decade or so later, in 1604, Shakespeare wrote another play – Othello. With the persona of the More, Othello, he does practically as much harm by cultivating society's uncritical, spiteful and hateful attitudes towards this alien non-European. The character of Othello represented the alien, a man of colour and an Arab.

The above are just two easily identifiable fundamental flaws in the works of the great playwright, William Shakespeare - as he is held to have been in his time. Over three-and-a-half-centuries afterwards, the world in 1986 had a new distinguished playwright – this time from Africa.

Passing time, in this discussion, is supposed to lead the reader to expect that any subsequent product should be higher/better in quality or ethical value than the one of the same kind preceding it – to humanity. The producer or inventor then earns recognition for the improvement thus made. Like Shakespeare before him, Professor Wole Soyinka's elevation to the Nobel Prize Laureate level exposed him to being critically evaluated on the basis of the same human issues of intolerance, rejection, discrimination and the like based on racial, cultural, religious or other differences. Can it be said that living four centuries after William Shakespeare, Wole Soyinka, in his literary works by the year 1986 contributed towards greater or better sobriety in a manner that constituted a significant improvement on what had been served to humanity by William Shakespeare? In order to answer this question - positively or negatively one should base his position on concrete evidence taken from Professor Wole Soyinka's public written or orally made utterances that are available to the world and particularly to African literary minds or general readers.

Of particular relevance in this regard are the publicized exchanges between Professor Wole Soyinka and another well-known African controversial Kenyan Professor, Mwalimu Ali Mazrui[13]. In those exchanges, Professor Wole Soyinka rejects the latter's assertion of being an African. To Professor Wole Soyinka, Ali Mazrui did not qualify to be an African, and he, therefore, rejects him as an alien to the continent. This is Professor Soyinka's stand and message to the rest of Africa and the world, even though Ali Mazrui has always considered himself African, was born to a black African woman in February 1933 in Kenya and a Kenyan (therefore an African) father, albeit of Arab origin.

The views strongly and publically propounded by the Nobel Prize Laureate on this subject are grave with far-reaching implications for Africans and the world at large. If, according to Professor Wole Soyinka, Ali Mazrui cannot be an African, then what is Africanness? The rejection of a person or an individual who himself confesses to belong to a place, and a given human society where he was born and raised and to the race of one of his parents is troubling. The person so rejected does not have to be an Ali Mazrui. What is at stake in this matter is the principle of belonging. It is a serious matter of denial of a well-established international human rights norm recognized under the 1948 Universal Declaration of Human Rights. It could be any other person or group of persons.

---

13 **Insert here the exact publication where the debate between these two personalities exchanged arguments**

If Professor Wole Soyinka's way of thinking were to be followed, several individuals, including the President of the United States, Baraka Hussein Obama and Nicholas Sarkozy, who was President of France till May 2012, to mention just these two, should never have been allowed to have access to the American and French nationalities in the first place since the American and French people should have rejected them. In the same vein, the twenty thousand persons or so of Asian extraction whom President Idi Amin rejected as aliens and expelled from Uganda in the year 1972 had no case to argue against the decision by the Ugandan authorities that rendered them stateless even though for many of them the only country they knew in the world was Uganda.

If followed by Africans in dealing with the political differences, Professor Wole Soyinka's thesis would mean that former South African President Nelson Mandela miserably failed by embracing Mr Frederik Willem de Klerk as a compatriot and, therefore, fellow South African instead of rejecting him. Historians will undoubtedly argue in the future that such was the message the great African thinker and celebrated playwright in our time sent out in his exchanges with Professor Ali Mazrui. Others might even further argue that it was such an attitude that African leaders in places like Ivory Coast – namely Laurent Gbagbo- emulated in later years when the latter introduced the concept of "*Ivoirité*". Adopting the attitude of "you cannot be one of us" and finding justifications for it, Mr Laurent Gbagbo embarked on the policy project that stripped scores of persons of their nationality, although the same people had been citizens of Ivory Coast until then. With the sudden introduction of new genealogical criteria to be met by the country's inhabitants, Mr Alasan Watara, a former Prime Minister in the country, was one of the immediate primary victims of that 'rejection inspired policy'. The results include the civil war, which ensued and culminated in the absurd political confrontation and the military showdown that ended in Mr Laurent Gbagbo's capitulation, capture and ending up behind bars under the International Criminal Court of Justice. Openness, tolerance or brotherhood was not part of the message.

Although a world distinguished thinker, Professor Wole Soyinka's message let down many on this point, less talented political leaders on the continent could be pardoned for utterances of that kind. The needed light and direction which humbler beings badly need and expected from him did not come.

Writing and discussing issues of mutual human understanding so many years after William Shakespeare did, Professor Soyinka's teaching and message ought to have reflected better and further foresight. In fact, comparatively, William Shakespeare could be partly pardoned for his moral or ethical myopia that led to the poisoning of his contemporaries' minds – as he probably had no idea at the time of writing the two plays mentioned above that the stuff with which he entertained European people would, three hundred years later during the 1939-45 World War result in the gas chambers where thousands of Jews would be annihilated under Adolf Hitler's Nazi Germany.

Of course, man's propensity to hate and reject another has had justifications of all kinds in different contexts. The minority white population in South

Africa reduced the non-white indigenous inhabitants to sub-human beings or totally denied them recognition as fellow human beings at all[14]. With notices such as BLACKS AND DOGS NOT ALLOWED in public places, one did not need to look for clearer evidence of this dehumanization and rejection of the other. At the time "South Africanness" was a status only white persons could qualify for, and blacks were herded into caricature "nations" apart - referred to as Bantustans. Officially adopting the apartheid legal system in 1948, South Africa had been denounced by most African peoples and non-African nations with a conscience. Under the "colour bar" rules of racial discrimination, persons were admitted or rejected based on the colour of their skin. The cost to Africa and most notably to the South African autochthon peoples in terms of human lives, suffering through torture, imprisonment, humiliation and material deprivation over four and half decades from 1948 to 1994 defies any measurement. For this reason, Nelson Mandela's decision not to reject or expel the country's white inhabitants on becoming President stood in sharp contrast to the message sent across Africa by the 1986 Literature Nobel Prize laureate. Gracefully, Nelson Mandela, too, in 1993, was awarded the Nobel Prize[15].

---

14 The recognition of Saartjie Baartman as a human person and obtention of the removal of her remains from a museum in Europe where it was treated like any other wild animal species did not occur until the racist regime of apartheid collapsed and Nelson Mandela as the President of South Africa pressed the people of France into repatriating South Africa's unfortunate daughter for appropriate burial in her homeland.

15 Nelson Mandela was awarded the 1993 Nobel Peace Prize for his work for the peaceful termination of the apartheid regime, and for laying the foundations for a new democratic South Africa. "... a shining example for the world that there are ways out of the vicious circle of violence and bitterness", Chairman of the Norwegian Nobel Committee Francis Sejersted said in his speech at the award ceremony in Oslo, Norway. (Source: http://www.nobelprize.org/nobel_prizes/peace/laureates/1993/mandela-wall.html)

Rejection of man by man has also arisen where skin colour or the so-called race difference is not the issue. The tragic fate of the Jews in Nazi Germany or the horrors visited on the black African population under the apartheid regime in South Africa had parallels over time in other places, painfully including several of them in Africa. Thinkers and political leaders, particularly those regarded as possessing "exceptional talent", have a duty to engage in critical interrogation - from an African standpoint - over the apparent absence of thought on critical issues to people's togetherness and survival. In judging the quality or value of cultural and literary products, Leniency may be expected where the work analysed is by ancient thinkers. Within the African context, the cases under consideration are hardly half a century old. Evaluating our present thinkers or politicians, who are our contemporaries, cannot benefit from the same leniency. It is an obligation to be more demanding. Unfortunately, signs of not being adequately circumspect in thought and somewhat lax in time management seem to characterize even Africa's supposedly best brains.

In concluding this reflection devoted to humanities, it appears as though successive intellectual products by the said highly talented persons have failed to improve earlier ones. With his extraordinary talent, William Shakespeare was blind to the fact that he was entertaining his European contemporaries with lethal hate stuff. Although doubtlessly a rarely gifted playwright and poet, Wole Soyinka too seems to have failed to see that in taking the position he did about Ali Mazrui's Africanness - and by the same token many others like

Mazrui, he was sending a message of intolerance and rejection. Compared to William Shakespeare's writings, his work brought no improvement upon the flaws in the latter's. The irony is that in terms of 'added value' inherent in thoughts expressed, Professor Ali Mazrui delivered a powerful message of inclusiveness and even global brotherhood in taking the stand he defended.

III

TURNING WESTERN ARROGANT IMBECILITY INTO AFRICA'S GODSEND WAKE UP CALL

This chapter cites instances in which Africa has publicly been abased by Western leaders or Western civilisations at large. It proffers means by which this belittlement can be taken in stride by African nations, and used as honest criticism Africa can reflect on to solve her own problems.

D iplomacy often faces resistance because some people consider its entire cultural set-up as a form of institutionalized hypocrisy. Once, at a drinking event, Koubalou had to respond to a pointedly impolite question when an interlocutor wanted a *yes* or *no* answer to the assertion that: *Diplomats are people paid to lie for their countries abroad.* Koubalou, surprisingly and without apparent hesitation, answered *yes*, but with a request to explain this self-incriminating response. He pointed out that English is unfortunately a complicated language in which the same word, especially in its oral form, can mean several things. He gave the example of the word **male** (/ˈmeɪl/) that cannot be phonetically distinguished from **mail** (/ˈmeɪl/ l). Going back to expound his affirmative answer, Koubalou explained that to lie, for him, meant going to bed and therefore lying down every night abroad in the service of his country. This meaning of the phonetic form of the word *lie*, (/ˈlaɪ/) is the one he had opted for.

On 11 January 2018 a crude utterance emanating from the President of the United States, shocked the entire African continent. Mr. Donald Trump used the uncouth disparaging word "shithole" in describing the countries of Africa, Haiti and El Salvador[16].

---

16   https://www.theguardian.com/us-news/2018/jan/12/unkind-divisive-elitist-international-outcry-over-trumps-shithole-countries-remark

US diplomats around the world were summoned for formal reproach, amid global shock over Trump calling African nations, Haiti and El Salvador 'shitholes'

Donald Trump has been branded a shocking and shameful racist after it was credibly reported he had described African nations, as well as Haiti and El Salvador as "shitholes" and questioned why so many of their citizens had ever been permitted to enter America.

Photograph: Jonathan Ernst/Reuters in *The Guardian- International Edition, Front page, Friday Jan 12 2018 - Trump suggested the US should bring more immigrants from Norway, not 'shithole countries.*

A storm of reactions from numerous corners of Africa erupted after that unprecedented and provocatively offensive phrase which the Head of State of the United States used.

It's not the storm which Mr Trump's rude language aroused from Africa which catches our interest here. Rather, our curiosity is about understanding why anyone on this earth could describe Africa as a *shithole*! Is it possible that rather than entirely putting all the blame on the rude person who chose the insulting language, Africans should in fact concentrate on asking "why did this man describe our nations in this way?". Is it possible that the point is simply about the choice of words used, while the nations are in fact conditions which Africans themselves know to be inescapably embarrassing?

The central issue at stake may be simply stated: do Africans know that the bad-language that was used represents a reality on the continent, but reject any utilization of such grotesque language while talking about another person's nation? On this central question relating to Africans' own view of the continent, the modern enslavement and slave-selling widely reported on in the international media, caused a President to challenge colleagues on the ineptitude displayed among many fellow African leaders:

> "If we allow others to define our problems and take responsibility for solving them, we have ourselves to blame. A major pillar of institutional reform of the AU is a more focused and assertive Africa."[17]
>
> *(President Paul Kagame addressed fellow leaders in Dakar, Senegal, at the International 4th edition of the Forum on Peace and Security in Africa)*

The human haemorrhage of defenceless and often unsuspecting persons attempting to escape pervasive poverty, famine and disease in many African misgoverned nations, is a terrible open abscess on the continent's world image in this age. Many African leaders, hats in hand, consistently run to Western nations to beg for subsidies and assistance, even where the European/Western nation being begged is truly less

---

17   http://www.africanews.com/2017/11/13/africans-are-to-blame-if-others-define-and-solve-our-problems-rwanda-s-kagame//

endowed with resources. One should for instance take the contrast between a country such as Japan on one hand, and Congo DRC, or even between Switzerland and Uganda. The table below will help if one wants to see the comparison between the four nations at a glance[18]:

Table 1: List of Countries by Projected GDP Per Capita
Source – link in footnote 18

Nation Name	Area/ Km²	GDPp/c /K$	Population millions
DRC	2,344,858	474	81,339,988
Japan	377,930	38,282	127,484,450
Uganda	241,550	686	42,862,958
Switzerland	41,284	78,245	8,476,005

(Area of Japan = 16% of Congo DRC. Japan feeds more than 8 times the people in DRC.

Area of Switzerland = 17% of Uganda. Switzerland has less than $\frac{1}{5}$ Uganda's population.)

Japan which is only 16% of the landmass of the Democratic Republic of Congo has an average yearly earning capacity per single citizen, of over US$38,000. In the DRC, the figure is below US$500.Similarly, Switzerland whose total area is only 17% that of Uganda has each individual citizen producing an average of

18   http://statisticstimes.com/economy/countries-by-projected-gdp-capita.php: List of Countries by Projected GDP per capita, International Monetary Fund World Economic Outlook (April-2017)

more than US$ 78,000 per annum while the figure for Uganda is only US$686.

When uncanny outsiders like Mr Trump utter such insulting bitter truths about the comparatively sorry state of the African continent, it should not only shame Africans, but should become a necessary and useful irritant to force Africans from their irresponsible slumber. If taken this way, President Trump's distasteful sentiments about Africa could prove an unexpected blessing in disguise.

The Reality of African Abasement Amidst Global Advancements

Today the world is truly a global village because of the phenomenal technological advancements. Whereas history records that it took four months for Columbus to travel from Europe (Spain) to what is today the Dominican Republic in central America, in the year 1492[19], travellers today require only a third of a day – i.e. about eight hours - to cross the Atlantic from e.g. London, Europe, to New York in the USA. This is also true when traveling between Europe and Africa, as seen by Africans today. People can compare things with a fresh mind between environments in African places and outside the continent. Many know that Mr Trump is wrong to be so blatantly disrespectful, but the same people will often agree to the truthfulness about what is wrong and inadmissible at home.

19 http://www.history.com/this-day-in-history/columbus-reaches-the-new-world

The general situation in many African countries, is reflected from the poor salaries (if) paid, to law enforcement personnel such as the police, customs officers as well as immigration staff that ensure corruption becomes the order of the day. Health facilities and equipment, as well as medication that patients should receive, are dysfunctional or simply no longer in existence. Avoidable deaths occur in their hundreds while schools – where they exist - have overcrowded classrooms lacking reliable, qualified teaching staff and basic materials such as text or exercise books. Added to the above is the level of poverty that is coupled with very high costs of living and unemployment.

It's against this background that one could explain people's preparedness to take the high risks of consorting with criminal operatives who smuggle them out in their hundreds of thousands, only to end up as corpses in the Mediterranean Sea when their unsafe boats capsize, or in Libyan slavers' detention cellars. This absurd reality in Africa is now well documented by media houses such as CNN, Aljazeera and others for anybody in the world to see and hear. Africans decry all this, but are ineffectual in pushing those in power to do anything. Sadly, rampant corruption allows some individuals in high political positions to turn a blind eye to all the criminal activities going on, or even to collude with the criminals.

When the above conditions prevailing in very many African countries today, are compared to the law-abiding environments such as those prevailing in most European or Western nations, one cannot help to be concerned about the fate of the ordinary citizens who live in Africa. While it was insensitive and spiteful on the part of President Donald Trump to use the blunt language he employed in describing the countries, the point was brutally made. Many self-respecting Africans may not want to be referred to in the way the American President did, but inwards the utterance was a welcome shock that leaders in Africa needed in order to look at themselves in the mirror. Will Africans learn from this embarrassment?

Shamelessness and/or clumsiness is not very African. Generally speaking, most societies in Africa inculcate a culture of politeness, obedience, as well as respect for elders, to the point where individuals grow up scared of questioning the established order of things. While modernity has penetrated Africa through churches, schools, and open mass media, its significant impact on the youth has not taken away the persistence of some old cultural attitudes and practices. Fortunately, there is real competition between the two forces. It must be this confrontation between Western and traditional African cultural approaches, that the brings contradictory reactions to Donald Trump's rude utterance on Africans, from Africans.

When the above is properly understood, the fury sparked off by Donald Trump's uncouth comment assumes a two-sided meaning. Some reactions denounced the American President in a language just as barbaric! This should be understood as Africans displaying astonishment to the crudeness exhibited by the Westerner, moreover from such a high office where courtesy should be at its highest level. The attacks may have been less against the salacity or exactitude of how he described African nations! What shocked the average African most profoundly, was the impudence.

The language Donald Trump used was felt to be uncultured[20]. It was all an outrage at the utterance. The clash in this regard was culturally understandable for people who are familiar with cross-cultural proficiency.

African Fragilities

The strong reactions from Africa to Donald Trump's rude remarks also stemmed from other reasons. Some of these were racial. World history records very long nasty experiences lived by persons of African origin – particularly in the United States of America, Latin America and in the Arab world where they were subjected to enslavement and discrimination. For a white person, in this day and age, to be as insensitive as Mr Trump sounded, inevitably constituted a form of reopening old wounds. The counter attacks from Africa did not need to be out of a cultural difference. The issues here were of a political nature. Coming from the high office of the President of the USA, Mr Trump's vulgarity seemed to indicate it was the American people as a whole were insulting all Africans. That is totally understandable when it is kept in mind that Africans have not overcome the feeling that white people suppressed and often brutalized their forefathers until only about half a century ago. Intelligent and careful westerners in their dealings with African people

---

20 http://www.thesaurus.com/browse/uncultured

normally keep that ugly recent past in mind. Mr Trump did not show any intelligence in this regard.

A third category of Africans who reacted to Trumps blunt description of Africa, Haiti and El Salvador, constitute of a significant part of well-informed though often discrete and apolitical men and women. These people, regardless of their country of birth or residence, find the leadership in place frustratingly inept, opaque, and corrupt. They see themselves as passengers on a train about to crash, because of the state of mind of the crew, and the dangerous mechanical condition the train has reached – not to speak of the horrible stench emanating from the toilets as well as the bar wagon. It is night time on this train. There is no lighting as bulbs burned out or were removed and never replaced. Drunkards and all sorts of thugs, thieves and rapists move about unchecked and the atmosphere is frightening. It is in the midst of this that a frank and fearless passenger screams out insults directed at the proprietors of the dangerous train.

Like Mr Trump, the crude speaker offends the owners of the train. The crew gets angry and if only they could get their hands on him! The rest of the passengers inwardly totally agree with the courageous isolated voice but their disgust with the conditions in which they are is unsaid.

The loud-mouthed passage who screamed out his frustration and insulted the train owners said the truth – facts which everybody on the train was witnessing and suffering from. From this shaming of the operators of the train, they might decide to do something about it in the future. The criticism of those holding positions of power is not tolerated. Those who take the risk of saying anything uncomplimentary to the authorities, see themselves severely sanctioned, including being imprisoned for life. In order to be safe; prudence, surrender, and caution become the mode of life. It is these suffocating conditions in many African countries, coupled with very high unemployment figures, that explain why so many unsuspecting youths fall victim to criminal syndicates, and end up being smuggled to even greater misery abroad. It's from this stand point that calling the nations concerned **hellish** or, to use Mr Trump's phrase "**Shithole**" may be considered brave, constructively frank, or even called for.

The anger, embarrassment and reactions caused by President Donald Trump's infuriating attack on Africans, cannot leave thinking Africans indifferent. The remark may have been a timely prick on the African politicians' dependency syndrome balloon, which must start to be deflated. Politicians who habitually turn to USA and Western powers hoping for economic hand-me-downs may, after the public slap and spit in the face by a white man, think twice. Does a beggar expect those donating to him/her to treat him/her worse than a dog? Doesn't a beggar expect to be treated as a fellow human? Africans will never praise Mr Trump for his brutal and humiliating remarks of African nations, but those remarks will have some unexpectedly positive consequences in all circles – political, academic, cultural and social.

This chapter is based on a paper that was presented as a contribution to the debate Africans must engage on, in the future the continent wants to see.

IV

AFRICANS IN FRANCE (EUROPE)

*This chapter is based on a paper that came as a sequel to two major contributions towards the clarification of the issue of Africans as a people: Firstly, the inspiration to embark on this discussion stems from an expansive documentary produced by Professor Ali Mazrui in his 1979 BBC Reith Lectures series under the title 'The Africans'. In that unprecedented undertaking on the peoples of Africa, Ali Mazrui raised the critical question, 'Who are Africans?' And responded to it in several unorthodox ways. The debate sparked off by those views, continues to rage across the African continent. The second source of inspiration was an even earlier, equally monumental and controversial research project, which was developed under the directorship of Lord Hailey whose initial work commenced, ironically, in the year 1933 when Ali Mazrui was born, and entitled **An African Survey**. Other than an indirect and oblique recognition of Cheikh Anta Diop's*

*revelations[21] added to the colossal research by Chancellor
Wiliams, an African-American Scholar[22] on the African-
ness of ancient Egyptian Pharaohs, stimulation to embark
on this subject comes from the numerous discussions and
interactions with Africans, as well as with indigenous
French people over approximately three decades spent in
metropolitan France as a legal alien of African ancestry.
The French have the saying, 'Chacun voit midi à sa
porte[23]'. Professor Ali Mazrui developed the theme for his
lectures at the close of the '70s while residing in the United
States of America. In this regard, he was, and still is, part
of the African diaspora there, unlike this author who is
currently situated in France. If the above French saying
holds, our perception of an African and how the African
experiences things in France may not exactly depict the
impression people elsewhere have. In fact, the criteria used
in defining 'the African' in the context of France may also
differ considerably from those which Professor Ali Mazrui
or Lord Hailey utilised in their gigantic surveys. In our
case, the parameters of time (epoch) and space (location),
a particular individual's race, as well as cultural and
political convictions are taken to be critical in considering
the African in France. Based on these criteria, an attempt
is made to define an African in this specific context and
to clarify what is meant by France from a historical and
geographical perspective, i.e., in terms of time and space.*

---

21 Nation et Civilisations Negres, 1979

22 The Destruction of African Civilisation, 1971

23 This could be indirectly translated into English as 'People don't see things the same way. What you see depends on the position from which you observe something.'

Definition of Africans

The definition of an 'African' can be understood based on the stand point Lord Hailey adopted and reflected upon in his statement, about the objectives which the different European colonial powers fixed themselves, in adopting particular approaches or policies to do with governing their subjects. This was purportedly done in all cases in order to civilize or develop Africans. Basically, unlike Britain, France allowing Africans within her national borders from the very day she acquired her first colony Senegal (Saint-Louis in 1673) in the wake of Europeans' 'discovery' of the new world – the Americas. This approach leads the reflection as far back in history as around the year 1452, when Pope Nicholas V issued Dum Divers - the Papal Bull that granted Emperor Alfonso V of Portugal the right to 'reduce any Saracens **pagans and any other unbelievers to hereditary slavery**' (bold emphasis is mine). This was a significant milestone as the French settlers, like all other Europeans in the West Indies, needed manual labour, and found Africa to be the ideal source of this commodity i.e. slaves. Since Africans slaves were considered as property to those who bought them, this is the date that tends to be conveniently cited as the earliest encounter between Africans and the French. However, I disagree with this assertion, as expounded in the subsequent paragraphs.

First of all, Africans are not just those indigenous inhabitants of the continent south of the Sahara. To confine African-ness to this portion of Africa would be to argue that the painstaking scientific work of Sheikh Anta Diop, Chancellor Williams, and Lord Hailey on the African-ness of Pharaoic Egypt that was subsequently vindicated by many other archaeologists in the Soudan, was meaningless. Indeed, Lord Hailey considered it necessary to explain the practical operational constraints which prevented his team from covering the countries in Northern Africa. Our approach takes the whole of the African landmass into account, discussing Africans in the manner with which Professor Ali Mazrui did in his work. With this approach, it is possible to see the first encounter between the people from the north of Africa and the French at a different time in history. The Berbers, Nubians and Arabs who have lived north of the Sahara Desert for millennia, i.e., the Egyptians, Tunisians, Libyans, Algerians, Moroccans and Mauritanians, cannot be excluded from the people we call Africans. This position rejects the alienation of the inhabitants of the northern part of the African continent. It is this same position, moreover, which was taken by great Africans like Kwame Nkrumah (in his pan-African pursuit) and later reinforced by Professor Ali Mazrui's assertion regarding the question of African-ness: nearly three decades after his 1979 BBC lecture series project, he gave a keynote in 2008[24]. Along Cheikh Anta Diop's lines of thought, we must go back to pre-Islamic times <u>and even far beyo</u>nd, to trace the shared history records

24 Prof Ali Mazrui PUBLIC LECTURE. October 23, 2008 at 6:07 AM <B> Pretender to Universalism: Western Culture in the Globalising Age</B> Keynote for the Royal Society of Art and the British Broadcasting Corporation, to be delivered in London, England.

of Ethiopians (Africans), Yemenites and Saudis (Arabs) over Queen Sheba who lived about 1000 BC. Clearly, blood commonality existed between Africans and Arabs, and was concretized in the person of Emperor Menelik I of Ethiopia, the son of Queen Sheba and King Solomon. Since then – over 3000 years ago – the present interactions between Arabs and Africans in Eastern Africa, the Middle East and the northern parts of Africa, are an undeniable basis for both the biological and cultural fusion of these peoples. These Afro-Arabs were living together when Islam as a religion came about. It should follow that the Islamization of the people in the region was not due to the introduction of Arabs in North Africa. Certainly, the spread of Islam was not a mission by Arabs only since it was only with the passage of time that natives in the modern-day countries of Egypt, Algeria, Tunisia and Morocco, became speakers of the Arab language.

To make a parallel comparison in the involvement of local populations in a process started by aliens, the story of British colonization in Uganda is good to cite. The British agents arriving on the north eastern shores of Lake Victoria (then locally known as Nyanja Nalubaale) first met the Kabaka (King) of Buganda who was at war with the Mukama (King) of Bunyoro Kitara. Their first move was to make a deal with the Kabaka and gain the support of the Baganda. Once this was achieved, the British gradually built on the 1900 Agreement which made the kingdom, Her Majesty Queen Victoria's protectorate. From that time on, the Baganda became chiefs, missionaries and teachers in the subsequent parts of what is known today as the Republic of Uganda. This is how Luganda is probably the most popularly understood and spoken language in the country, while English is the official language. Unfortunately, it is not the lingua franca below a certain elite level of Ugandans. One may argue that the British colonized Uganda unaided by the indigenous Baganda people, just as the history of northern Africans would have us attribute the conquest of southern Europe to 'Arabs' without the involvement of Africans! However, even though they are generally referred to as simply 'Arabs', the fact that these people adhered to the Organization of African Unity in 1963 from the very start is testimony that they see themselves as Africans. Regarding the perception which other Africans may have on the inhabitants of northern Africa, a boy born near the southern tip of the continent in 1942 made a forcefully instructive statement 70 years later that truly reflected the fusion of the sentiments of Africans to the south and north of the Sahara:

> 'In this context we should recall the impulses which, during the last century, resulted in the convening of the Pan-African Congress and the formation, before the birth of the OAU, of the 'Casablanca bloc' to which, to the best of our knowledge, Tunisia, Egypt and Libya belonged.'

There is very little doubt that Africa's great minds such as Kwame Nkrumah Osagyefo, Gamal Abdel Nasser Hussein, Ahmed Sékou Touré, and Muammar Muhammad Abu Minyar al-Qaddafy, who departed long before him, would have shared this sentiment regarding the analysis given today by one of Africa's most read and acknowledged political thinkers, Professor Ali Mazrui. This fusion goes deeper and beyond mere ideological discourse. It is also biological in both the distant and recent history of Africans. President Anwar Sadat of Egypt was born of a black African mother and Salim Ahmed Salim, who served the longest as Secretary General of the OAU has a mixed Afro-Arab parentage. This partly answers the question, 'Is Ali Al'Amin Mazrui an African?'

To conclude on this argument of whether or not the inhabitants of North African are Africans, let us ask the following question from a geographical view point and try to answer it individually:

> '…if Madagascar, the Comoros and Mauritius, that are 1829, 530 and 2637 kilometres away from the African continent respectively, consider themselves to be part of Africa, what is the basis for excluding and de-Africanising the inhabitants of the northern part of it too?'

The First Africans in France and Legacy

With the question of African-ness for the inhabitants of north Africa concluded in that manner, the discussion of 'Africans in France' takes a dramatic leap backwards into history as far back as the year 1455 cited earlier to about seven centuries before it, i.e., the year 719 AD – when 'North Africans' conquered southern Europe bringing large parts of Spain and southern France under their control, and ruling them for over four decades –

probably ending with the Battle of Tours in 732 AD although their real withdrawal from the battle is said to be around 752 AD by some historians. It is held that these invaders (Arab North Africans) were driven by a religious passion and the desire to spread their faith to all lands within their reach – and France happened to be one of these. Roger Garaudy, a controversial European French philosopher and writer, in his book cited above, quotes one of France's outstanding conscientious philosophers and politicians, Anatole France, who in his book *La Vie en Fleur* literally makes a lamentation over the departure of invaders from his country (Gaul) in 732 AD after the defeat in Tours:

> 'Mr Dubois asked Mrs Nozière which was the most fatal day in French history. Mrs Nozière didn't know it. It is, said Mr Dubois, that of the battle of Poitiers when, in 732 AD, Arab science and civilization ceded ground to the barbarity of the Franks.'

Those North Africans had lived as masters and had introduced a different way of life, in many ways expanding the then existing level of knowledge. They brought advanced science (in medicine, physics and mathematics, architecture, agriculture) and humanities – basically a new form of civilization – to France. It is quite possible that the defeat and expulsion of those Africans (Arabs) from France after the battle of Poitiers, was a setback in the progress started in the different domains that were interrupted. Patriotic French citizens ensured that the positive acquisitions from that alien rule continued to grow and were subsequently improved upon.

Africans forcefully entered France, lived in a position of authority, and decided on how society should be organized. Ironically, these would be exactly the reasons, according to Lord Hailey, the European colonial powers state would use to justify the colonization/occupation of Africa! This is a cruelly ironical argument. If the people of France were entitled to reject the claim by North Africans at the time that they positively contributed to the human condition, the same French people place themselves under the obligation of recognizing the legitimacy of the denunciation by Africans a century or so afterwards, when the former claim that their colonial occupation and cultural assault in Africa from the mid-19th century to the present was useful. Otherwise, invaders are often both a curse and a blessing, if Africans and the French were to go by John Milton's English idiom that 'every cloud has a silver lining'.

The first Africans in France of the early to mid-eighth century, left inescapable evidence of well appreciated contributions to metropolitan France. At the time, human development in the areas of culture, societal or political organisation, as well as in basic scientific advancement, appears to have been at a much higher level among the inhabitants of Africa than it was in France. Traces of new words originating from Arabic, the principal language used by the North Africans, are numerous in the French language today. Many European and French writers, as well as historians, have done research which shows that Africans in France contributed to the advancement of this country's original inhabitants. Africans in France, however, would have other experiences in the intervening centuries as will be shown later on in this discussion.

As would be expected, France resisted the intrusion of Africans from North Africa as alien masters. Several reasons can be given to explain the attitude of the French. One of the strongest and culturally disturbing of these, was the imposition of Islam, on a mainly Christian people. The religion Africans brought to impose Islam, was not only different but was also in some aspects, based on diametrically opposite doctrinal beliefs, such as banning the consumption of alcohol (incidentally a word derived from Arabic chemistry) and wine in France. This new religion, in fact, sought to replace Christianity itself. In medieval Europe, France was held as the Vatican's eldest, and perhaps, most faithful daughter. In other words, if the Vatican in Rome, the seat of the Pope, was the mother of the Church, the totality of France's devotion to Catholicism was so definite that no other European nation could compete with her. This 'Catholic-ness' of the French people as a nation is essential to the understanding of the experience of Africans in France globally. In this context therefore, year 1452 when Pope Nicholas V issued his Papal Bull, becomes a milestone. French settlers, like all other European entrepreneurs, were establishing plantations in the Caribbean. After the decimation of the indigenous populations on the 'pacified' islands, the settlers discovered that they required manual labour. The answer was found to be the hunting, capturing and shipping of Africans across the Atlantic Ocean, as slaves. It was this business that the 1452 Papal Bull blessed and even urged Catholic France to enthusiastically pursue!

It is an old customary practice in international law that sea vessels are extensions of the national territory of the country whose flag they fly.

Africans in France Overseas (Africans as slaves)

Africans, therefore, once captured and dragged, to the island of Gore off the coast of Senegal or Elmina in Ghana, from which they were tied hands behind and chained. Even before the boats left the port, they were in France. For these unfortunate Africans, being in France commenced from the point of entering the French owned boats, which were bound for the Caribbean Island colonies across the Atlantic Ocean. Most of them died before reaching the destination. Roger Garaudy estimated their average survival rate to be at 10%.

The trans-Atlantic slave trade was to flourish until it ran into the determined resistance and ultimate successful rebellion of African slaves in what was then known as French Saint Domingo, now present-day Haiti. For over two hundred years (1626 – 1848), therefore, Africans in France elsewhere would continue to exist as simply property or objects, maintained in a condition not different from that of mere beasts of burden like bulls or horses, which are at the mercy of their human owners. Thankfully this condition, for a number of reasons, did not reduce all Africans in France to submission. We hold the view that an acute sense of self-respect, refusal to accept the sub-human status to which European masters sought to reduce them explains the resilience of Africans in bondage.

In fact, the point that large numbers of human beings who were being treated like animals captured from the jungle, had been ripped from highly cultured societies in Africa and taken mainly from the zone where today's countries of Nigeria, Ghana, Ivory Coast, Senegal, Guinea, Mali and Benin etc., are situated, explains the indomitable human power. Regarding codes of social and political conduct, these were societies which had formally laid down rules such as those contained in the Kurukan Fuga Charter, codes on human safety and harmonious co-existence[25], dating back to over two centuries prior to the eruption of savage societies from Europe with sophisticated weapons, hunting for fellow humans whom they failed recognize as such.

It could be argued that slavers from Europe were incapable of recognizing Africans as human beings like them. Denying Africans the status of fellow men by Europeans, was followed by mixed expectations from the latter. If Africans were sort of beasts of burden like buffaloes and bulls in Asia, the treatment they received on the plantations followed that logic. Yet, there was cruelty which owners of horses or mules, camels and donkeys normally never subjected their animals to. In a sense, Africans were treated as human beings on the basis that they were expected to understand their masters' instructions with unquestionable obedience, i.e., behaviour not based on reasoning was required of them. The slaves must have found the treatment they were subjected to by the European Christian owners, to be shocking and savage. If one knows Article 24 in the Kurukan Fuga Charter mentioned above, it solemnly

25 The Charter of Kurukan Fuga (According to the Epic of Sundiata Keita, Kouroukan Fouga or Kurukan Fuga was the constitution of the Mali Empire created after the Battle of Krina (1235) by an assembly of nobles to create a government for the newly established empire.)

stated: 'Never harm a foreigner.' One cannot help making a quick mental comparison between this phrase from a 'primitive and savage' Africans' Charter and the 'civilized' Pope Nicholas V's edict with its supposed godly infallibility – since the Pope was Christ's own representative on earth. And this was two centuries after the Kurukan Fuga charter!

It can be deduced from the ensuing observations that on the whole, some Africans in France at that time had as much deep self-respect and pride as they did despicableness of their tormentors, though it caused the latter's infuriation, which resulted in wild behaviour. This is another reason for the resilience exhibited by Africans as slaves. When absurdity exceeds its limit, it produces unexpected results. In 1759, Voltaire dramatically captured the slaves' destitute condition in his novel, *Candide*:

> '…a Negro stretched on the ground with only one half of his habit, which was a kind of linen frock; for the poor man had lost his left leg and his right hand.
>
> "Good God," said Candide in Dutch, "what dost thou here, friend, in this deplorable condition?"
>
> "I am waiting for my master, Mynheer Vanderdendur, the famous trader," answered the Negro.
>
> "Was it Mynheer Vanderdendur that used you in this cruel manner?"
>
> "Yes, sir," said the Negro; "it is the custom here. They give a linen garment twice a year, and that is all our covering. When we labor in the sugar works, and

the mill happens to snatch hold of a finger, they instantly chop off our hand; and when we attempt to run away, they cut off a leg. Both these cases have happened to me, and it is at this expense that you eat sugar in Europe;...'

This gross dehumanization of Africans in France under the conditions of slavery did not leave Jean-Jacques Rousseau, another contemporary great political thinker like Voltaire, indifferent. For his part, Jean-Jacques Rousseau denounced slave trade and slavery unequivocally, in such scathing terms as to declare that a slave who killed his master committed no crime in law:

'Giving up ones freedom is to give up one's status as a man, the rights of being a human being, in fact even one's duties... It is easy to demonstrate that a slave who kills his master commits no crime by doing so - neither by natural law nor by the law of the people.'

Recognition of the extreme conditions of African lives in France away from the Metropolitan territory, did truly strike some men and women of conscience in Metropolitan France. This can be seen not only through the writings such as those by the two great thinkers above, at the time. A very important radical woman and human rights defender whose name remained obscure for over two hundred years, but deserves special mention here is, Madame **Olympe de Gourges**.

This was a fearless anti-slavery heroine who publicly denounced the establishment for its duplicity over the horrors of slavery. For her audacious views, Olympe de Gourges was arrested, tried and executed in November 1793. Today, Olympe de Gourges is recognized in some feminist and women rights advocacy circles as having been a forerunner for the cause of women's rights in the world.

The story of Olympe de Gourge shows this duality of the French society. It is capable of initiating the grandest and best of human ideas or inventions but at the same time displays the most objectionable human modes of conduct. When this is fully grasped, one is in position to appreciate the dilemma Africans in France were faced with at any given time. There were slavers determined to continue with the cruelty in the colonies and yet in Metropolitan France, there were some people with such deep conviction and determination to champion the case for the freedom of African slaves. France has always been a place of surprises and some of them are truly extraordinary. One of these is that France was the first of all the West European countries to abolish this cruel and inhumane trade in humans by law, in 1664 while all the other European nations continued to legally enrich themselves through slavery!

What has been said above should have taught us that when he issued the *30 Floréal An 10* on 20th May 1802, Napoleon Bonaparte abrogated the law of 4th February 1794 according to which the National Convention had re-affirmed the abolition of slavery in French colonies.

This duality in the attitudes which Africans met in France came into sharp focus at the beginning of the 19th Century with the case of an African woman, Saartjie Baartman, who arrived in Paris in 1814 when France was under Emperor Napoleon Bonaparte, only to die under wretched circumstances a year later. The description of Saartjie's experience from various sources reads that this African '…was exhibited in Paris by one Henry Taylor and then by someone called Reaux. By the time she died, she was owned by an animal trainer…' and further that '…Sara was literally treated like an animal. There is some evidence to suggest that at one point a collar was placed around her neck…' After she died, her entire skeleton, brains and genitals were displayed in the National Museum in Paris for over 150 years until 1974. It wasn't until after the fall of apartheid that the late President Nelson Mandela raised the issue of the repatriation of the remains of Baartman with the Government of France, in 1995.

It is the duality of French attitudes in the experience of this African in France that saves the image of France, showing it as a society with a human soul too. But before, for well over a century and a half, the denigration of the Saartjie had continued. First of all, the country which epitomized the equality of all human beings, the fraternity and solidarity in the world, objectified a person while she was alive by reducing her to an animal and object of gaze. After she died, her remains were turned into mere guinea pig laboratory materials and museum collections, in the way animal carcasses or trophies are treated. Gracefully, France could not be insolent when Nelson Mandela raised the issue with the late President François Mitterrand. In spite of the vehement opposition from notable figures such as Baron Georges Leopold Cuvier, the racist scientist who dissected her after she died and the likes of Professor Henry de Lumley, who as president of the National Museum, remarkable French personalities like Senator Nicolas About and Roger Gerard Schwartzenberg, the research minister, ardently argued in parliament and ultimately evoked article 16-1 of the Code Civil Français (C-cF). Based on Bio-ethics Law No. 94-653 of July 1994 on respect for the human body, for Baartman's remains.

> Thus, it is this same France which decided:
> '...that justice be done to Saartjie who was subjected during her life and even after, as an African and as a woman, to offences resulting from long-prevailing ills – i.e. colonialism, sexism and racism...'

Africans in France, particularly in the colony of Santo Domingo which was France's most profitable property in the West Indies, were incensed by the reversal of the provisions of the Revolution according to which white supremacy and slavery had been abolished. The law Napoleon introduced was seen as a negation of their inalienable rights as human beings within the Republic i.e. the 1789 Revolution acting as the basis for their demands.

While this question was settled in Metropolitan France, it turned out to be a home-grown political catalyst that threatened to destroy the country's most lucrative business of the time – the sugarcane and tobacco plantations – with the slave labour that sustained them. The white settlers chose to thwart the slaves' rebellion, which necessitated military backing from Paris. Emperor Napoleon Bonaparte, having authorized slavery anew, lent support to the businessmen and planters, in the interest of national commercial gain. The African slaves clung to the sacred principles enshrined in the 'La Déclaration des Droits de l'homme' and valiantly fought Napoleon's army. Under the leadership and command of General Toussaint Louverture, the Africans succeeded in fighting off the nationalist French army, leading to the creation of the first ever black Republic in 1804 – Haiti.

The troubles stirred up between settlers and slaves where the latter made up the bulk of the population in the colonies, did not confine themselves to Haiti. In order to enforce the existing republican law passed by the Nationale Convention of 4th February 1794, Paris had to dispatch a military contingent to l'Ile de France (modern day Mauritius) and to la Reunion, that was tasked with securing the rights of the black population still under the settlers' subjugation there. The contingent arrived on the island in June 1796, but was rudely repulsed, leading to a volatile situation which was only stabilized with Napoleon's law officially allowing slavery. This time, France actually went to war against settlers **in defence** of the Africans – an act which should be noted and praised. This rescue mission was a failure, in spite of its noble intentions. Professor Ali Mazrui would have called this a 'heroic failure' in the way he described Julius Nyerere's economic failure during the 1970s in Tanzania.

The situation of Africans in France during the 17th, 18th and 19th centuries clearly shows that even at that time, they were living different experiences of life, just like the rest of the French people. Slaves in

Santo Domingo rebelled because France had declared the Human Rights for all people with the Storming of the Bastille. It would be interesting to know why the Africans in Saint-Louis, Senegal did not react in a manner similar to those in Haiti. This is where this discussion must now turn towards the Africans in a different kind of France i.e. in Africa.

Africans in France in Africa

Africa became of critical commercial/economic importance to European imperial powers during the 19th Century as the enlightenment gained ground, and technological advancement showed that machines were a preferable alternative to human or animal power in the exploitation of nature. In confrontations where European masters had to quell irate and rebellious African slaves by the use of guns, swords and other instruments of cruelty, it became clear that humans could frustrate their businesses by setting entire crop farms or stores of harvest on fire, damaging tools, etc. In contrast to these high risks, machines once maintained in good mechanical order, guaranteed results and profit. Slavery therefore, gradually lost the original attraction it had in the planters' and manufacturers' eyes, leading to the abandonment of slave trade and slavery itself. The anti-slave movements may have played a part too but a more critical assessment brings out evidence to show that it was mainly the commercial risks involved that significantly weighted in favour of discontinuing slave labour.

France had developed considerable commercial and industrial projects, of which Haiti was one of the most lucrative. The loss of that territory and the threat posed by competition from other European nations to rip other territories in the Caribbean, the Indian and Pacific Oceans away, forced France to find alternatives for her survival like her neighbours Britain, Spain, Portugal and Germany. The African continent became the new theatre where this age-old competition among European colonial powers took place. It is from this point that the relevance of the assessment done by Lord Hailey on the objectives and policies in conducting actions, and the consequences of European colonization of Africa, assumes its full importance in this discussion.

In her justification for occupying her areas of influence in Africa and ruling the inhabitants living there, France stated that it sought to 'bring civilization to the primitive and savage societies' of the 'dark' continent. The undertaking was presented in the most humane and philanthropic terms, where white men were to take on the burden of turning the brutes into some semblance of human beings – a task that could see its citizens risk being harmed and even cannibalized in the process. It is not part of this discussion's objective to prove whether or not the Europeans' stated purpose was called for in Africa. Rather, like the purpose of Lord Hailey's survey is stated, one should be interested in establishing whether the activities engaged in by the colonial rulers actually led to the realization of those stated goals.

French establishment of colonies in Africa roughly followed this order: Senegal (1626 -1659); Mauritius, initially Isle de France (1715), Algerian territories (1830 -1848). According to French historian Mathieu Guidère, when the Ottoman Empire under which most Arab states in North Africa belonged became weak, France launched wars against Tunisia by imposing the status of protectorate over it in 1881, and finally made Morocco its protectorate in 1912. The war to subdue Egypt had been raging since 1798 as part of Napoleon Bonaparte's imperial ambition. Then came the creation of 'l'Afrique occidentale française, AOF' over most of West Africa – i.e. l'Afrique-Équatoriale française (AEF) consisting of the colonies of Gabon, present day Congo, Chad, the Central African Republic – formally Oubangui-Chari) from 1910 to 1958 with the Governor-General based in Brazzaville.

French colonial rule in Senegal started with the four communes (towns) of Saint-Louis (1673), Gore (1677), Dakar (1857), and Sufisque (1859). According to the French constitution in 1848, Senegal was run under the same rules and regulations as any part of Metropolitan France.

All these territories and the African people living there, once brought under French rule, were legally part of France, and were destined to ultimately become integral parts of metropolitan France. Lord Hailey shows that France's stand on this quite clearly:

> 'The goals of the civilizing endeavour accomplished by France in the colonies exclude any idea of autonomy or any possibility of evolution except within the framework of being part of the French Empire. The idea of creating self-governments in the colonies, even in the far future, is to be ruled out.'

How Africans in this 'France in Africa' were to take things, becomes a key matter for us to examine. There is abundant evidence to show that despite the declared humanitarian intentions on the part of the French, Europeans' settlement was resisted, probably because occupation was almost invariably preceded by terrible wars to subdue natives, traditional political authorities or structures, and to forcefully impose French control. Negotiation was very rarely used as a method for arriving at arrangements of co-existence between settlers and the indigenous people. Moreover, France adopted a policy of cultural assimilation which aimed at producing not just 'humans' from the primitive inhabitants, but specifically French persons in the Eurocentric sense. Professor Ibrahim Wani elaborates on this point:

> 'The French colonial policy was assimilationist, and its primary objective was to turn the Africans in their colonies into French men and women. Education in the French African colonies, for example, was designed to rapidly produce black French men and women...The goal of French colonial policy then was to progressively elevate the African from his primitive surroundings into the French way of life. Africans who became assimilated by emulating the French way of life, by becoming proficient in the French language and by learning to appreciate the finer points of French culture became French citizens.'

The consequences of this policy in terms of the mentality it produced among those indigenous people who had access to that 'civilizing' process of education, were considerable. Professor Wani further observed for his part that,

> 'Africans from the English-speaking world cite Senghor's embrace of the French language, for instance, as evidence of the pervasiveness of French influence on Africa. The point...is the extent to which the Africans in the former French colonies view(ed) themselves as French rather than Africans, or at the very least have acquired French culture at the expense of their own.'

This process produced more than one kind of 'Africans in France'. Before seeing the divergent kinds of Africans the process produced, it will help to know the cultural and political basis on which the policy of assimilation was founded.

The French probably meant well in seeking to give what they genuinely believed in; the excellence and the superiority of their culture. The corollary to this conviction, however, is that the French were either unable or simply unwilling, to recognize the existence of any form of culture or civilization among Africans – not even in the form of language. This became the beginning of the annihilation of native or indigenous cultural values.

We hasten to point out that this was not an attitude held by French Europeans alone. It was the manifestation of a state of mind which almost all

Europeans shared. In his survey cited earlier above, Lord Hailey reported:

> '...in 1932-1934 two members of the Kenya Medical Service published a certain comparison between the brains of Europeans and Africans, in which one compared their cranial capacity and the other the characteristics of the cells of the pre-frontal cortex. The results were accepted in some quarters as evidence of the inferior mental capacity of the African, but recent studies of the brain have failed to establish any correlation between cranial capacity and mental intelligence.'

Interestingly, the report continues:

> '...it is noteworthy in this particular connection that Eskimo, Javanese and some Bantu tribes return higher averages of cranial capacity than the French or English...'

This view, that Africans needed to be guided and civilized by the European superior race until they could be brought to a level of intelligence to live as fully developed human beings, is traced to two influential writers of the early 20th Century – namely Professor Lucien Levy-Bruhl from France, and a Belgian Catholic Missionary, Placide Tempels who later served in Congo (present day Democratic Republic of Congo). The result is that these ideas were in some cases, absorbed by African intellectuals during the colonial era, therefore that belief in the teachings inevitably manifested itself in subsequent years. Different Africans ended up developing divergent perceptions of who they really were. This dichotomy in the philosophical perception of 'self' among Africans in France assumed crucial importance as will be dealt with in greater detail when comparing the mind-sets and attitudes of outstanding Africans in subsequent years. This divergence came out most clearly over the concept 'negritude'. Suffice to say, some African scholars still consider that, 'The basis of French assimilation was the supposed superiority of French culture and the corresponding inferiority of African culture.'

From the onset, some Africans vehemently objected the philosophical basis that French cultural teaching in Africa was a form of denigration of the African person and human worth. Furthermore, these 'Africans in France' considered it an arrangement where the best an African could become was a second-rate French person instead of being himself – a true African. There were Africans, however, who saw their gradual transformation (improvement?) through the system the colonial rulers, as a privilege to be enthusiastically grabbed at in order to ultimately be 'elevated' to the rank of 'les évolués' and hopefully qualify for full 'French citizenship'. The latter kind of Africans in non-metropolitan France was best illustrated by individuals such as Leopold Cedar Senghor, Felix Houphuët Boigny, Bernard (later Omar) Bongo, Jean Bodel Bokassa and others. It may be said without fear of contradiction, that all these men emulated one very exceptional slave descendent from the French Guyana colony, Felix Eboué. This black Frenchman rose to great heights in French colonial administration by being appointed the first ever, black French Governor in Guadeloupe and later to Chad in Africa itself where he served as an 'African in France' on the African continent for twenty years.

However, contrary to the above examples, was the famous Frantz Omar Fanon, also a black African descendent of slaves in Martinique. Basing on his strong political convictions, like his fellow black African Felix Eboué from French Guyana, Frantz Fanon moved to Africa to join the nationalist resistance movement for the liberation of Algeria from French colonial rule. Ironically, as a governor in Africa, Felix Eboué had for his part joined General Charles de Gaulle in the 1939 French resistance against German occupation of France during World War II while consolidating French colonial occupation in Africa. It can therefore be seen that 'Africans in France' presented and still continue to present not just a single type. Consequently, in discussing the question about who an African is and how that African lived in France, many parameters come into consideration. It is for this reason that we draw a comparison of some prominent personalities from the first African country where France established a colony, namely, Senegal. For purposes of comparing and contrasting, however, cross-references will be made from time to time between this country's experiences and others.

The results of France's political and cultural assimilationist policy in Africa, particularly prior to the '60s – when many colonies became independent – are that many Africans who, although on the continent and well after the former colonies had become independent showed very mixed, and at times even diametrically opposed attitudes towards France. Of the French colonies in Africa, Senegal produced some of the most striking examples of this ambivalence in attitudes. Three outstanding names stand out both domestically and internationally, as highly reputed intellectuals and political opinion leaders. These renown 'Africans in France' are: Leopold Sédar Senghor (1906 – 2001); Amadou-Mahtar M'Bow, (1921-) and Cheikh Anta Diop (1923 – 1986). There is no doubt that the three men grew up and lived as French Africans, both in the colony and in metropolitan France, probably receiving the best kind of formal education possible at the time. A close look at their individual appreciation of what it was to be an 'African in France' shows that some real differences existed. Our focus here will be mainly on their intellectual and philosophical persuasions.

The eldest of the three, Leopold Sédar Senghor exhibited a rare kind of admiration for all things French throughout his life. Yet the irony is that his name has been so closely associated with the concept of 'negritude' and the pride which it is meant to carry for African blackness, that some even mistook him for having 'coined' it. On closer examination, however, one discovers that he was only one of the earliest converts to this cultural ideology which he met in Paris, of which the veritable origins are traceable to 1885 in Haiti. Prior to this, available information suggests that the originator of the concept 'blackness' was the Haitian anthropologist, Anténor Firmin.

Senghor is particularly remembered today among African intellectuals and political analysts in the Francophone countries as a thinker, poet and political leader. Additionally, as his country's political leader 20 years after independence, he left a profound imprint on Senegal's national character. The impression he left as 'an African in France', however, is highly controversial, and a considerable number of thinkers continue to denounce his apparent espousing of a theory propounded by racist colonial anthropologists. This is to the effect that Africans, being primitive and uncivilized societies, had inferior intellectual capacity and operated on the basis of emotion, intuition and myths as opposed to brains, objective reasoning or logic – unlike the developed and civilized people of the white race. Virulent criticisms emanated from prominent contemporary thinkers and politicians such as Cheikh Anta Diop, Ahmed Sékou Touré, and Aimé Césaire (a very close friend at one time) who are now all dead. However, one well known and respected Senegalese personality who is still alive must be added – the former Director General of UNESCO, Amadou Moctar MBOW. The latter is the African who, during his tenure of the above office saw to the re-writing of *The History of Africa* in eight volumes by mainly African scholars of repute. Even those who understand Senghor's personal views as having been driven by his extraordinary desire for accommodation among all human societies (universalism?) and seeking to create a world culture that integrated 'negro' values with those from the white race, have said this of him:

> '… In its majority, the African intelligentsia does not recognize itself in Leopold Sédar Senghor, nor does it consider him as a leader. No terms are harsh enough to fustigate his pretended imposture. Helter-

skelter L.S. Senghor is accused to have underestimated black men's capacities of adaptation.'

Another member of the African Francophone academia from Cameroun would express more or less the same reasons for his scepticism during an interview on Senghor, the poet:

> *Question* – 'Basically, what do you reproach Senghor for as regards his negritude?'
>
> *Reply* – 'Senghor conceived culture as something biological and considered black men as being emotive. These two theses posit that if we are biologically more emotive and that we cannot transcend this emotiveness, we therefore are condemned by history. In fact, Senghor did not hesitate to conclude in explaining that white domination over black people was logical and natural.'

In reaction to Senghor's philosophical leaning and political style, Ahmed Sékou Touré, another contemporary African in France, in the neighbouring colony of Guinea and who also became head of state in that country upon becoming independent had the following observations over Senghor's presentation of African-ness or blackness:

['The mystifying ideology of imperialism
(...) tricked the African in order to steal
his continent, and yet, here is the African
himself, via his negritude, accepting to
assume this dispossession. This slave
became a negro, this negro, turned into
a slave admits: "Yes I am a nigger, I have
the soul of a nigger, I am unreasonableness
and unconsciousness (...) As for us, we
assert that no consciousness could be
white, yellow or black (...) the values of
civilization, the reasons behind history
and the conditions of men's existence are
defined by the social or anti-social nature
that appertains to it and not by the race.
The African can and must affirm his
human values without having recourse to
irrationality.']

Analysts have suggested two major kinds of the concept
'negritude'. The Senghorian –'*négritude senghorienne*'
largely explained by his wholesale submission to the
ideas which two influential writers of the early 20th
Century, namely the French Lucien Levy-Bruhl and the
Belgian, Placide Tempels. Indeed, the phrase which has
fetched so much harsh criticism for Senghor, concerns
his perceived self-abasing stand on African culture and
philosophy. Senghor's perception of the African literally
encapsulates the theory propounded by these two
anthropologists. For him it is apparently an accurate
description of Africans and other non-European

peoples: primitive, brainless and therefore having no capacity to think or reason:

> 'Emotion is Negro as reason is Hellenic'
> or in French, '*L'émotion est nègre, comme la raison héllène*'.

It is against that background that a different appreciation of 'Africans in France' must now be presented. In contrast to the impression Leopold Sédar Senghor left of an 'African in France', one should also consider the experience of other illustrious persons who, like him, lived at the same time, had the same education in France – first as colonial subjects in Africa, later in Metropolitan France and finally as citizens of an independent African country in France. We shall compare Léopold Sédar Senghor with Sheikh Anta Diop first. It would not be an exaggeration to say that Anta Diop as an African in France, held views that were diametrically the opposite to Senghor's, although both men were intellectual authorities on African-ness in different fields.

Professor Thierno Bah in a comparative article on the two great pillars in African thought writes the following of Cheikh Anta Diop:

> 'It is in a social and intellectual context hostile to Africa, that Cheikh Anta Diop's trend of thought develops. Born (...) in a small village in Senegal, (...) very early while in high school, he is confronted with debilitating ideas about races. Those written by Voltaire, Hume, Hegel, Gobineau and Lévy-Bruhl who all worked so hard to

legitimize the comparative inferiority of the black people to that of the whites on moral and philosophical grounds. Africa would then be subjected to the horrors and violence of European colonization – societies which continued trading in slaves started in the 16th Century. The vision of an Africa devoid of a history, whose inhabitants, the blacks, never produced a single element or sign of being civilized was then disseminated within minds and through written works.'

This African in France, unlike his compatriot whose ideas smoothly aligned themselves with those propounded by his colonial masters, mentors and others, found little to enjoy but lived a life of intellectual confrontation and exclusion that culminated in his rejection. Professor Thierno Bah continues:

'It was in order to fight this falsification of history that Cheikh Anta Diop through thorough investigation of History, Egyptology, Linguistics, Anthropology, Philosophy, and Physics, endeavoured to put into question the basis of occidental culture as related to the very genesis of humanity.'

From the start, Cheikh Anta Diops thesis, having been refused by the **Doctors at the Sorbonne** (emphasis mine), upset the intellectual establishment's tranquillity by demonstrating with near irrefutable arguments that the ancient Egyptian civilization was black and African, and by recommending the decolonization of African history. The objective was to free the history of African societies from the colonial prison, by means of a Pan African discourse.

For the rest, the difficult relations between Senghor and Anta Diop, as well as the incompatibility of their views over Senegal's political history and intellectual life, are well documented. Rejected in Metropolitan France for his non-conformist intellectual views, Sheikh Anta Diop was to be barred from holding a teaching post for 27 years in his own country, Senegal, until President Leopold Sédar Senghor died. The problem is not simply an African's experience in France. The policy of assimilation sometimes de-Africanised the colonial subjects and created antagonistic mentalities within the same nation. The sharp differences between the experiences two Africans had in France comes out most strikingly with the fact that Cheikh Anta Diop was denied recognition as a powerful and thorough brain for his pioneering thesis on Egyptology, by the supposedly great intellectual gurus at the University of Sorbonne. It surprises some that while this was so, by the time he died, Leopold Sédar Senghor had been decorated with the rare honour of becoming a knighted member of 'L'Académie Française'.

In conclusion of this comparison, the last of these three distinguished 'Africans in France', Amadou Mahtar M'Bow will now be considered in terms of how his attitude related to that of Senghor. Like the first two men, Mahtar M'Bow's life transcended colonial France,

France of the Second World War times, and Post-war France through the years of nationalist demands for independence, that finally led to this extremely divisive question regarding Africans in France on the continent: Would they, in a post-independence Africa, choose to remain in or go outside France?

For brevity, we shall refer to a speech which Amadou Mahtar M'Bow made on June 26th, 2006 during a special colloquium under the auspices of the *Organization Internationale de la Francophonie.* While the speech was intended to be part of the homage paid to Senegal's first President who is generally held by the French as a model of 'an African', Mahtar M'Bow does provide revealing hints on how and where he and Léopold Sédar Senghor considerably differed on many political and cultural issues. Even though Mahtar M'Bow states that the rapture in their companionship occurred in 1958 over the referendum question, this seems to have been an important culmination of the difficult relations the two personalities must have been having all along. Indeed, Mahtar M'Bow adds, they would remain politically estranged for eight years from that date until 1966.

It is clear from the quotations Mahtar M'Bow attributes to the pre-independence nationalist struggle days Léopold Sédar Senghor that for the latter, independence could not be envisaged outside the French Imperial patronage and tutelage. Imperial France had to be the framework under which Africans, on attaining independence were to place themselves. Mahtar M'Bow explains what Senghor meant:

'And he gives a rough idea of this imperial community: The colonial nations would be constituted on the basis of the existing federation... The Governor General, appointed by Metropolitan France would alone have executive power and the right to take initiative in matters of legislation... An 'imperial Parliament' would be located in metropolitan France where the representatives of metropolitan France and of the colonies would meet. This parliament would deal with all questions of general interest: Imperial Defence, Foreign Affairs, etc...'

The above conception of the power arrangement with the Governor representing Imperial colonial authority at the top, shared by some elected African elites posed very serious problems for many enlightened Africans. Here, the two camps to which each man belonged, is evident. Like Sékou Touré in neighboring Guinea, Mahtar M'Bow must have voted against the form of 'independence' Sédar Senghor sought to have under France.

At the cultural level again, an utterance by Sédar Senghor seems to be a contradiction of his confessed beliefs, and certainly something that the 'self-conscious' African Mahtar M'Bow wouldn't take since it stood as a clear subordination of the African cultural values, practices and institutions to those of the colonial master. It left the impression that whereas the master did not have to adopt African ways, the African would have to absorb the French civilization:

'...It's out of question that metropolitan France adopts the indigenous customs and institutions. Nevertheless, France should understand them (…) It is particularly for the colonies to imbibe the French civilization…'

Mr Mahtar M'Bow goes on to further to make his departed companion say very kind words about colonial France:

'France may be a country of well off - middle class people. France has never been racist. France is the least colonialist of all 'colonialist' powers.'

Yet later in the same speech, citing an occasion which he describes as having been the very first time Senghor uttered the word 'independence' as far as his memory could go, M'Bow clearly stated his bitterness over French racism and political imposition:

"Not exactly, because I would like to conclude in reaffirming to white people our unshakable readiness to gain our independence and that it would be foolish and dangerous for them to reverse the course of things. We are prepared, if necessary, as the last resort to regain our freedom by whatever means, including even violence. I don't believe that France which has just got rid of Hitler's racism would blame us for such a decision."

In fairness to both men, at least on this point as Africans in France, they shared the same view. This comes out clearly in the words Mahtar M'Bow spoke after quoting his compatriot:

> 'I can say today that this cry from the heart, at the moment he made it was shared by a great many of us African students who had just been demobilized from the Army of Liberation in France after the war, and with quite some difficulties, it must be said, to pursue our studies - we who had offered our lives for the freedom of the people of France if it became necessary (…) The trust we had that it was possible to live a common life in freedom, dignity and progress was being cruelly tested by the hesitations and regression from vested interest ready to sacrifice the future in order to preserve privileged positions which they held only because of their situation as ' settlers', and which in their eyes gave them a superiority justified by nothing but race.'

It becomes possible to conclude that Africans in France, even under the colonial era when some of them were accorded a special status within the empire making them French citizens too, viewed and reacted to daily issues in considerably varied ways. This has been graphically illustrated by three highly enlightened citizens of one colony, Senegal. Of course differences such as those observed in the attitudes of the nationalists in Algeria as a whole, and that of the colonial subjects in places such as Ivory Coast, Guinea or Gabon, etc., demonstrate similar interesting outcomes of the colonial occupation on different societies

But what is the present situation? It is to this question we now turn.

Africans in France Today

Discussing Africans in France today is the trickiest part of our reflection. For this part, we have chosen to limit the period from 1981 to 2013. These two dates delineate a duration which coincides with our own uninterrupted residence in Metropolitan France as legal alien Africans, attentive to happenings around us. The year 1981 is a French historical landmark that deserves special mention. In that year, a country within the NATO group of nations brought communists into a government that had been democratically elected for the first time, coming to power with the French Left led by François Mitterrand, the victorious Socialist Party candidate with which they had formed an alliance. Previously, leaders of the French Right tendency had dominated political power since General Charles de Gaulle after the Second World War. Interestingly, after the two-term presidency by the Socialist Party under Mitterrand for over a decade, the Left was defeated and effectively kept out of power for nearly two decades. Ideologically, France oscillates and for Africans in France, this is not without repercussions.

Generally, an African in France today could rightly consider himself to be an extremely lucky person on earth. This is because of the very balanced blend of state authority and the people's liberty in terms of economic, social and cultural rights. This is particularly true about the 'Hexagon', or Metropolitan France. It is also in this geographical part of France that most of the Africans in France considered in this chapter, live. For the purposes of this discussion, we shall divide Africans into four categories: 1. Africans from Francophone countries or former French colonies. 2. Africans born on French soil, regardless of their parents' origin. 3. Africans who came to France from countries that were not colonies of France, and finally, 4. Africans temporarily living in France as international civil servants, businessmen, diplomats, or students. The number of Africans as tourists in France is not big enough to justify a category for special consideration here. It may also be noted that although Africans fall into the above categories, reactions from French people can significantly vary depending on whether an African is from the south of the Sahara or from the northern part of the continent. This latter categorization may sometimes go hand in hand with one's being a Christian or Muslim. It may be relevant to mention here that an important formal association Le CRAN (Representative Council of France's Black Associations) exists in France.

Africans in France from Former French Colonies

In Metropolitan France an African is common to see, but difficult to classify along the lines given above.

The African in France who comes to mind right away, is a manual worker in Paris who is in France because an agreement exists between his country and France according to which work permits may be accorded to a number of non-French persons to do jobs for which there isn't too much competition in France. This arrangement is of mutual benefit to the two nations, and also for the individual. These Africans are mostly male, blue-collar employees. However, arrangements for enabling their spouses or close family members to join them are sometimes possible. Once this happens in Metropolitan France, the chances that the couple start bearing children are many.

This category of Africans is almost exclusively from former French colonies. Very limited previous schooling and sometimes very little command of the French language coupled with illiteracy (some can write and read but only Arabic) characterize these persons. Their dress code tends to remain as they had in the villages back home in Africa. Culture is what they know in their communities at home. All the above characteristics of this African in France only constitute a striking, if not strange appearance for some time. After staying in France for several years or decades, complications start to arise for the African in France where there was none before. A typical example is to take a couple from Niger, Senegal or Mali who starts a life as described above.

The couple manages to find the items for local food from the open markets. When a child is born, if it is a boy, circumcision is done either traditionally by a qualified tribesman, or in hospital. In almost all West African countries, every boy child undergoes this as a traditional requirement. The same applies to girls in from certain parts of Africa, except that the operation is not as simple or public like that of boys. Tradition requires that a girl child be cut in a certain ceremony commonly referred to as Female Genital Mutilation (FGM). This practice is prohibited by law in France; it is considered a barbaric act and a violation of the girl child's fundamental rights. This comes as a rude intrusion into the parents' private family lives where they start to feel that they are no longer in control of the children they bear! Soon after comes the requirement to take those children to kindergarten and later elementary school – regardless of whether it is a boy or girl child. By 10 years of age, children will have assimilated so much of the cultural values and practices unfamiliar to the parents that the latter start losing control. Only a few firm parents overcome this alienation and loss of power over their children. The location of the family's home may be a hotbed for high crime rate involving mostly low-income male teenagers. Delinquency, violence, drug abuse and rejection of institutional education are challenges that the youth, largely within the low income class, pose to their families. Many of these are children of immigrants from Africa.

These conditions undermine the results of the freely accessible low-cost educational facilities which France provides for all its children. Children may even start to see no role model in their parents. They start looking at their parents as less capable – speaking broken French, unable to assist them with even the simplest written homework – with the media fuelling furth portrayal of their parents as backward and behind the rest of the population. The children increasingly turn to other references for their material and intellectual development. A breaking point in these developments is reached when children threaten or actually decide to report the parents to the police or social workers for being forced to do certain things! Discipline is a word most kids in the streets detest in France. The children have increasingly grown into 'French' people, while the villagers from Africa often remain faithful to their old cultural values and practices. Issues of the generation gap and incompatibility between the old (parents) and the youth, become critical. Failure in life is feared by parents, while the children shout for freedom and liberty, in order to do what they want as individuals in a free-France.

The above scenario leads to the subject of Africans born in France and the kind of observable experience they display. The preceding two paragraphs emphasizes the importance of parents and the family environment in determining children's success or failure in school and the consequent social level these people end up belonging to as adults in society. The point is that children from middle and upper social class homes are favoured by the contribution the parents are able to make to their overall intellectual, cultural development – basic necessities for growing up – and successfully going through the education systems. Poor families or very deprived homes are not able to provide this support to their children in the same way. They lack material resources, knowledge itself and quite often aren't capable of providing a clear chart for the child to pursue for his future. As the majority of these children belong to the lower to deprived social milieu, most of them contribute to the perpetuation of this less than well off members of French society. Admittedly, some exceptions must be allowed to this general picture. There have been a few success stories too, one of which is Ramatoulaye[26].

It would be incomplete and unfair to only leave the picture of ordinary Africans in Metropolitan France illustrated above. There are simple but also remarkably foresighted parents who arrive in France empty-handed, but manage to socially rise to incredible heights. The explanation for this is apparently two-pronged: the idiosyncratic qualities of the individuals concerned (parents and children considered as individuals) and the extraordinary social security system which exists in France.

First, it is the quality of the person who comes to France or that of the individual child. If traditional African family and parental values are adhered to, the individual will seek to reach a higher social status through dedicated hard work, thrift, integrity and marriage. Such African men do everything to enable them to get a wife from home in Africa. This will normally lead to child bearing. 'Proof of real manhood' in traditional Africa requires that one brings up healthy and well-behaved children, capable of succeeding in their own life in turn. This entails constant conscious dedication to one's children from birth to maturity. When these are the guiding principles, even material deprivation does not necessarily prevent children from achieving the family's objectives. The close support from the father and mother through encouragement,

26 A Senegalese born girl who arrived in France at the age of seven, brought up by a single mother. She gravitates all the social ladders via good education up to becoming a minister in President Nicolas Sarkozy's government in 2007. In her French persona, however she changes her name to Rama Yade. She runs into problems and loses post.

guidance, and affection in these poor people's families, seems to be the first secret of success. Consciousness is growing among Africans in France.

The second explanation of success for 'second generation' Africans in France may be the extraordinary legal protective system - *la sécurité sociale* in favour of all families. An ordinary immigrant from Africa arriving in France, instantly finds that if they are a family unit with children, the state, on appropriately verifying the accuracy of the facts, will pay an allowance for every child per month, until 18 years of age. This support to the family increases substantially where the family has more than two children. Subsidized accommodation is likely to be found for such a *famille nombreuse,* while reductions on the fares paid when travelling using the National Railways Corporation (SNCF) and buses are facilitated. For people living in a country such as the US, this may sound incredible. The author has on several occasions wondered how many low income earners in the USA cope, in an environment where no equivalent of state run public transport exists. In France and Switzerland, many of the travelling citizens are on SNCF or municipal public transport. This existence of public services enables children, students, persons with disabilities, and the elderly (seniors), to benefit from reduced fares. This part of the French system has been sometimes abused by unscrupulous individuals who decide, for example, to have as many children as possible in order to maximize the amounts of money they can collect in child allowances! The idiocy sometimes gets pushed to the extreme by someone claiming to be a polygamist. In this case the individual (male immigrant) may claim several council houses in different towns around the country. With the possibility of presenting up to ten children or more, this becomes a tempting business strategy for some immigrants. Unearthing some of these criminal practices has led the State to increasingly impose stricter regulations which have come to include, for example, the interdiction of polygamy for people living in France.

Another extraordinary facility afforded to legal alien Africans in France, is free and compulsory schooling for every child. For most Africans to whom going to school was a mere dream, because access to schools depended entirely on whether or not one's family could afford to pay fees, it is a miracle-like privilege to have one's children born and grow up in France. This is a place where education is free to anyone who is capable and interested in pursuing studies up to university level, and sometimes even beyond. This is a fact which, knowing the difficulties the majority of parents and children still face in Africa, must be mentioned as France's gift to Africans who live there. It should be added right here that abiding with the law in matters such as paying taxes, which are expected of every able-bodied person, goes hand in hand with this human social paradise. True, there are complex existential factors which may prevent one from succeeding, but on the whole, one does not easily fail.

The above presentation of Africans in France has not covered those Francophone Africans who arrive with a considerable level of education or professional qualifications with which to integrate French society, and find employment at a higher social stratum. Their added advantage in this regard is just that they already speak French, while non-French speaking immigrants face that linguistic hurdle.

Professional Non-French Speaking Africans in France

The category of Africans in France which consists of people originating from non-French speaking African countries presents characteristics that make their entry into France complicated. In the majority of cases, they leave their home countries either by their own volition, or are forced by a variety of circumstances. They include asylum seekers, business people, and adventurers of all kinds including sportsmen, artists, etc. Some may even use dodgy methods to enter France. The life experience of these Africans in France can be anything from hilarious to tragic. We have known of two unhappy examples which are briefly described below.

Some professionals from various fields under Idi Amin's regime in Ugandan used to receive scholarships from the French Government to do specialized courses. Journalists, hoteliers, secretaries and post-graduate students as well as teachers, constituted this population. For some, this was a godsend as they did everything, once in France, not to return to their countries – probably an understandable option. With the known political risks and insecurity prevailing in Uganda at the time, the French often turned a blind eye to those who should have returned to Uganda at the end of their legal stay. Bravo, one might say, France Terre d'Asile

(France, land of asylum), indeed! But this was only the beginning of a long story for the individuals concerned.

Without sufficient command of the French language, these Ugandan Africans in France –young men or women who chose to stay – had serious difficulties penetrating the job market to become self-sustaining, on the basis of their professional qualifications. The end result was often that a former front manager or a chef in a big hotel in Uganda, for instance, became a simple chambermaid, waiter , or cleaner, if he or she was lucky! With time, youth and strength begun to wane, and the combined effects of alcohol consumption, severe winters, poor nutrition, and homesickness, took a heavy toll on them. The next thing was that the individual joined the desperate association of tramps on the streets or in the Paris underground.

However, the second kind of experience was in sharp contrast to the above illustration. There was a young Ugandan whose father was murdered with two other important people in Uganda in 1977. To save his life, he migrated to France and was granted political asylum. His father, previously the Chief Commissioner of Police prior to the Idi Amin regime, and appointed Minister of Lands and Water Resources, had a great talent for playing musical instruments. The son took after him and, while in France, started to develop that talent. It took the young man great initiative, patience and a measure of luck. He gradually gained public recognition, built a relationship with some French partners including a woman he later married and had a child with, and was a famous musician in France. Unfortunately in June 2018 he passed away, as a Ugandan, in a foreign land. This gentleman, Geoffrey Oryema, was a family friend of the author for years.

Lubaale mbeera nga n'embiro kwotadde (Aides toi, (et) le ciel t'aidera) – "God helps those who help themselves."

The French have a pertinent saying: 'Your rights will only be yours when you can demand and fight for them' – *Il faut revendiquer vos droits.* The Baganda in East Africa have a hilarious warning joke: *Bwosumagira tebabega*! This is translated as, 'If you dose, no food will be served to you!'. This seems to have always been true for the African experience in France. The French Revolution of 1789 declared liberty, equality and fraternity for all in France, but Haitians had to conduct a torturous and protracted war for years before they could wrench those rights from the French white plantation proprietors, who wanted to keep them in bondage. France offers great opportunities to aliens but success ultimately only results from personal capacities to imagine solutions, labour with sweat, perseverance and sustain faith in one's self. It is with this in mind that we should now move to the next part of 'Africans in France today'. An African who is from Buganda will do well to remind him/herself of the saying, 'Lubaale mbeera nga n'embiro kwotadde'.

Africans in contemporary France, just like those who lived here before them, are bold and ambitious in both the private and public domain. It can be said that of all the West European countries, France leads in her ability and readiness to include Africans among key decision makers in Government. Credit should be given to both the Left and Right of France for this quality. Central to these positive developments, however, are the determined, unwavering and vigilant efforts in which those Africans are deploying to first rise to the heights they are at presently, and most importantly, to remain there. It is not easy or a matter of being lucky. An examination of the African personalities who powerfully uplift the consciousness and confidence of Africans in France today, starkly brings this out.

For the first time in the history of France, Rachida Dati, a daughter of an immigrant African family with a Moroccan father and an Algerian mother, was appointed Minister of Justice and Attorney General on 8th May 2007! Furthermore, Mr Sarkozy in his election campaign made this African Arab woman his spokesperson. This was an extremely rare case considering this African woman in France is a Muslim. Very interestingly, Rachida Dati militated in favour of the ideals supporting of the 'Right' for ex-President Mr Nicholas Sarkozy who later commented:

'To the youth of France (…) with work and merit all became possible (…)'

There were two other African women appointed to ministerial posts by the conservative government when Mr Sarkozy's party won the elections namely, Ms Fadela Amara Fatiha, a daughter of an Algerian Kabylie large family, and Rama Yade (born Ramatoulaye), a Senegalese born naturalized Frenchwoman. What may be mentioned in respect to these three women is that Rachida Dati tended to downplay her Arab/African-ness in her lifestyle, at least publicly. This contrasts with Fadela Amara Fatiha who was publicly an Afro-Arab French personality. As for Rama Yade, she seemingly did not have to prove anything about what or who she is.

In all fairness to the three African women politicians whose loyalty was to the Right, each exhibited tremendous will power and tenacity in focusing on set objectives until they were attained. This did not necessarily win them friends among their colleagues or co-party members. Indeed, after each went through the warm initial phase as symbols of racial diversity and integration, their acceptability steadily went down until they were dropped, one after the other from the conservative government cabinet of ministers. Information available on the political past of each of these personalities reveals that in their past they had leanings to the Left. In fact, Fadela Amara openly declared her support for the Socialist Party presidential candidate in the 2012 elections. Rama Yade expressed her disgust towards President Sarkozy and his party by joining a breakaway group led by Mr Jean-Louis Borloo, another party member who became dissatisfied and frustrated by the President. It was only Rachida Dati who remained attached to the President until his unhappy end.

The outstanding performances by these three African women, should be contextualized by relating their experience to a related touchy subject which African-ness combined with womanhood and religious confession may sometimes lead to. In this regard, it is the French African from south of the Sahara, Ramatoulaye Yade who, in her own words, shows this unique status of vulnerability for an African:

> 'En politique j'incarne tout ce que les hommes politiques ne sont pas : une femme, jeune, noire et musulmane.'[27]

So far, this discussion has adequately shown that where brains, determination and confidence in one's self makes a person rise to any heights, racial and gender discrimination does exist to render the struggle harder for Africans. However, one's religion may at times become a considerably sensitive subject. Generally, and especially from the western world, France is held to be 'the birthplace' of human rights. The enjoyment of liberty, equality and brotherhood is taken for granted. However, it may be said that since the events on 11th September 2001 in New York, women – especially those from Muslim/African countries – have seen their personal free choice of dress curtailed. Regrettably, it is against the law for women to wear head gear that covers their faces – a normal cultural item for women from North Africa and the Middle East. This is a security precaution that was declared a policy, to prevent further terrorist attacks. The explanation given by the authorities for curtailing the freedom apparently makes perfect sense, if looked at from the public security's point of view. On the other hand, one has to understand that from a strictly cultural stand point, this is a true denial of the right which every person in France is entitled to. Ordinary law-abiding women who genuinely believe in the religious propriety of wearing the outlawed items cannot be simply ignored as victims of majority rule. Acquisition of legitimacy in international human rights

---

27 The equivalent in English is: Politically, I am the embodiment of all that male politicians aren't: a woman, young, black and a Muslim.

law by the minority groups is on the increase. However, this issue is in fact more complex than it seems. Simplistic statements often heard such as 'women are forced by men to cover themselves under Islamic religion' are not always borne out by facts in France. In this regard, credit must be given to France for its general adherence to the 'rule of law' in matters such as this debate over the extent to which secularism (*laïcité*) may be pushed to encroach on private life. The debate on the freedom of cultural rights continues but first of all means maturity of mind to enjoy entitlements.

What is fascinating is that, the Court of Appeal on 19 March 2013 pronounced the politically controversial decision of reinstating a Muslim woman who had been dismissed from her job at a nursery school in December 2008 for wearing a veil at work. The authorities of the nursery had won the case in a lower court against the female employee. The woman fought against the ruling until she obtained the reversal of the first judgment. What made this possible is the quality or independence of the judiciary in France. The State holds secularism to be sacrosanct – proscribing any religious symbols or practice. However, this law exists in juxtaposition with equally valued laws protecting privacy and the freedom for every person in France to believe in and practice the religion of his/her choice or in none. It is this latter part of secularism that the court of appeal focused on during its ruling of 19th March, 2013. The judge explained that the prohibition of practicing religion, legally applied in public institutions or services. This was not the case as the nursery where the woman worked and wore the veil as part of her religious practice was a private business.

This ruling raised unprecedented controversy involving condemnatory statements from both government ministers and the opposition parties directed at the Judiciary. Yet the simple woman involved, like many others who wear headgear such as the Burka, Niqab, Chador, etc., only do so because it is their sincere belief that this is the right dress-code. Often, there is gross oversimplification and reductionism in evaluating the African Muslim woman. It is not always true that women wear the veil in mere obedience to men. Like men, women do have the freedom to practice their religion as they judge appropriate.

With the French people's commendable and keen sense of cultural appreciation, it should be easy for society to appreciate the absurdity of forcing part of its members to abandon their cultural way of life. Under the right laws, everyone in France enjoys his or her cultural rights and this is what is proven by the recent decision by the courts.

France's Left, and the Experience of Africans in Public Life

As stated above, the Left in France also has Africans who deserve to be recognized for their tenacity, temerity, and capacity to fight. In the year 2013, the Socialist government had Counsellor Christiane Taubira, born in French Guyana. She is an accomplished jurist and highly experienced politician as France's Minister of Justice and Attorney General. Apart from her maturity, she is also proud to be a black woman, statesman, and outstanding intellectual.

If a number of tough Africans worked their way up into the conservative party and snatched appointments as cabinet ministers, it can be said that there is nothing particularly new about that. Black politicians from Africa have held ministerial posts since colonial times. Felix Houphouët Boigny, Leopold Sédar Senghor and others did it. What is new is perhaps the fact that today, these people are women which makes their posts exceptional. This should compel us to search for other novelties in Africans' experience of French public life today.

There are several other interesting signals that Africans in France are rising to increasingly make their presence felt, noticed and perhaps even clearly listened to. The regular rhythm of democratic elections every five years in this country and the possibility which this creates for alternating ideological teams in power enables parties – while in office – to introduce new or reverse existing legislation as they judge to be best suited for their party supporters. While parties are in the opposition, they tend to be less effective in this sense. What distinguishes a number of African French politicians on the Left, is the audacity they display in expressing what they see as unacceptable to them as a people of Africa descent. While it may be argued that one can equally militate for these same ideals from the conservative party, our own view is that the Left in France is a more enabling political environment where the kind of language the late Aimé Césaire used to use has space. The three African women mentioned above were not tolerated within the conservative party once they did not toe the line!

It may therefore be said that on 7th February, 2012 in the French National Assembly, the Socialist Party provided a platform for a (Member of Parliament) representing Martinique, Mr Serge Letchimy, of African descent to make a scathing criticism of the Minister of Internal Affairs over remarks the latter had made during a political rally, reportedly insinuating the superiority of some cultures (French and European) over the inferior others while obliquely suggesting those of the primitive or uncivilized races. The Deputy of Martinique expressed his objection to Mr Claude Guéant in such strong terms that Government Members in the House walked out in protest and demanded an apology not just from the person who uttered the words but from the Socialist Party as a whole. The following was the acidic criticism the French African made against the government minister:

> "…denounced therefore utterances that took people back to those European ideologies which led to the concentration camps coming after the long chain of colonial enslavement of people, asked whether the Nazi regime was a form of civilization and if the barbarism of slave trade, slavery and colonialism were a mission for civilizing others…"

This incident came at a time when the Socialist Party presidential candidate needed every possible voter's vote in France. As the party's Presidential candidate,

Mr François Holland should be commended for the courage he showed in refusing to apologize for what a member of his parliamentary group had said. The French nation's history had been dragged into the electioneering by the minister who did not expect that a Frenchman would challenge him so frontally and during an ongoing session in the national assembly. It will be remembered that all his life, Aimé Césaire, although a Frenchman, did not allow such effrontery to go unchecked. Mr Letchimy, who happened to be the successor to the recalcitrant Aimé Césaire expressed this view on the effects of colonialism are well known as exemplified below:

> 'They tell me about progress, about projects, cured diseases, standards of living raised beyond what they were. As for me, I speak of societies emptied of themselves, trampled cultures, undermined institutions, confiscated lands, destroyed religions, artistic magnificence reduced to nothing, suppressed possibilities. Facts, statistics of kilometres of roads constructed, canals, railways are thrown at me […] I talk about thousands of men sacrificed in Ocean Congo. I speak of those who, as I write, are digging the port of Abidjan with their bare hands. I speak of millions of people skilfully indoctrinated into living in fear, inferiority, trembling, kneeling, despair, boot-licking, barbarity…'

The people of France witnessed this outburst from Mr Serge Letchimy; as a nation they arbitrated and soon after elected François Holland's team in the elections. Indeed, only six months later, France would collectively make a huge gesture in this direction through its President towards Africa – Algeria in particular. The still unhealed wounds left by the colonial occupation of the African continent are well known by the enlightened people in France, especially towards the people of Algeria. The Algerians have never truly been made to feel that they were listened to, respected or that their pain, loss and bitterness was recognized by France. The French president travelled to Algeria and stood side by side with his Algerian counterpart during the events marking Algeria's 50th year of independence from colonial rule. President Holland on 20th December, 2012 made the following declaration to the people of Algeria in Algiers:

> 'For 132 years, Algeria was subjected to an exceedingly arbitrary and cruel system. That system has a name – colonization. And here I do recognize the suffering colonization inflicted on the Algerian People.'

The statement above can be taken as a sign that the president's entourage is having some positive influence on him regarding France's attitude and policy towards her former colonies in Africa. To appreciate this view, one may wish to compare the attitude and conduct previously displayed by President Nicholas Sarkozy on African issues during his term of office. One incident which crystallizes this contrast and which particularly infuriated the Francophone African elite occurred in Dakar, Senegal on 26th July, 2007. President Sarkozy went on to visit that country and had to meet the academia and students of the University named after the country's late great son, Sheikh Anta Diop. The French president made a speech that infuriated almost every self-respecting French-speaking African. To add salt to injury, Mr Sarkozy adopted a disrespectful attitude when he did not mention the name of Sheikh Anta Diop at any one time in his speech. In fact, Mr Sarkozy's speech was perceived as having been an intentional insult to the Africans. As if this wasn't unbearable enough for audience, the French president decided to praise the consequences of French colonialism in Africa, describing the continent as having no history and whose people needed to be awakened! Literally rubbing salt into the wound, Mr Sarkozy asserted that France owed no apology to Africa for what colonialism did. The excerpt below by Yveline Dévérin conveys the gist of that speech:

> The tragedy of Africa is that Africans did not sufficiently penetrate into history. For thousands of years, African peasants lived along with the seasons and the ideal for them in life was to be in harmony with nature. Thus, all they know is the eternal rebirth of time, and the endless repetition of the same gestures and the same words.
>
> In this imaginary realm where everything perpetually restarts, there is neither room for human adventure nor for any idea about progress. In this universe where nature commands everything, man

escapes the anguish of history that plagues modern men, but they stay motionless in the midst of an ever-changing order in which everything seems to be predetermined. Never do they aspire to a future. Never do they think of escaping this repetition so as to invent a future for themselves.

Numerous publications in response to what was seen as a misguided speech by the former president of France appeared in the subsequent months. While this discussion mainly presents views and reactions of Africans, it is useful to add that outstanding European specialists in the field did express their contrary views to those of their former president on the theory of what Africans are. 'Dosputatio' is a label placed on a publication entitled *L'AFRIQUE DE SAKORZY – Un déni d'histoire* co-authored by five academics namely, two Directors of Research in African History associated with France's prestigious CNRS (National Scientific Research Centre) and three outstanding African History professors.

Is there a shift in attitude towards Africans in France and could a French Obama be afoot?

Africans in France continue to contribute towards bringing about some changes, albeit rudimentary at present. This is observed in the approach being adopted by the new country's leadership in matters affecting

Africans locally and abroad. President François Holland recently declared that his government was not going to adopt a business as usual approach with regard to the 'Françafrique' network. He pledged to transform or even disband it. One should have also watched the preparations that were made for him to attend the International Organization of French speaking countries (or Sommet de la Francophonie) held in Kinshasa-RDC, between 13th and 14th October, 2012. There is clear and growing evidence that Africans in France are emerging on the scene as national political actors. We see this as being the result of the generally favourable interracial co-existence people in France have known for centuries now. If France practiced, like South Africa under apartheid or the United States of America as exemplified by the State of Maryland's 1664 legislation, which forbid interracial marriages, what Africans in France are witnessing and are in fact able to do today would not be possible. This is a credit the French deserve to be given, for all the shortcomings they may have, like all societies.

One of these indisputably positive signs on the lives of 'Africans in France' was the recent election and elevation of Mr Harlem Désir (originally Jean-Pierre Désir) a black man, to the highest position in the current ruling Socialist Party. This is the closest any politician within the French political tradition gets before being able to stand as a presidential candidate. Everyone is asking whether France is on the verge of witnessing a Barack Obama in a decade or less? But for starters, Africans need to know who this French politician is and if he himself sees himself as an African. Mr Désir, was born in Paris to a black father from

Martinique and a white French mother, a citizen of Alsace. Harlem (the name he willingly gave himself for ideological symbolism) has publicly and persistently identified with the less privileged and advocated for equal treatment of white and non-white French citizens. He has championed the struggle for humane treatment of people in difficulty while already living in France, regarding immigration law requirements. He is particularly known for having founded the successful civil society movement 'SOS Racism' in the '80s, a time when the extreme Right political party, the Front National, of Mr Marie Le Pen was formed and heightened racial discrimination and xenophobic behaviour in France.

Generally acknowledged as a rising star, first in his own Socialist Party, Harlem Désir has a much broader base of sympathizers for the typically republican French philosophy and ideals he stands for. His discourse spins on human rights as the fulcrum. He reiterates freedom, equality, and brotherhood in his relentless advocacy for a multicultural and multiracial France where a person's ancestry, race, religion or political views must not constitute a handicap. Although his defence for the less privileged sometimes rings so sharp as to earn him labels like 'black racist', he consistently declares his being a non-white French citizen himself, refusing to be drawn into racist postures or justifications; he simply states he is French, born in France and a child of parents from two races. He perceives immigrants as a potentially important source of national brain power and increased economic strength (provided that an appropriate attitude is adopted in France and equal opportunities given to all the youth regardless of their race or social class).

Arguably, this Frenchman with an avowed attachment to his father's non-white identity does have influence on the way other people in high political echelons view Africans in France. His operating style seems to be reminiscent of that which late President François Mitterrand described as 'la force tranquille' (or gentle power). He is credited for never being blunt or rude. He was vital to the Socialists at a time of dire need for internal cohesion and unity – during the last presidential elections. His rise to the highest office in the party must be seen as the fruit of tireless efforts to bring divergent views together. It is precisely this kind of quality that is required of a presidential candidate.

Is the African in France sufficiently critical of him/herself?

With the political horizon for Africans in France having been hinted at and seen to be rather promising, we must do an 'auto critique' to check whether the success or failure to realize the existing dreams are being seriously taken on by Africans. Are Africans engaging in any analysis of developments which are bound to affect their future – favourably or adversely in France? This point in this discussion calls for serious and focused reflection on the life experience of those Africans who lived in France centuries ago, recently as well as today. Kishore Mahbubani, the controversial Singaporean thinker who wrote a book entitled *"Can Asians think?"*

comes to mind here. Africans tend to be somewhat self-indulgent and should therefore find out more about this pertinent book. After reading it, I wanted to seek its author's permission to have it translated into French so that Francophone Africans may 'enjoy' it. On further reflection, however, a better idea occurred to me; that the word 'Asians' should be replaced with 'Africans' if permission is obtained to do so.

Africans' conditions in France or anywhere in Europe are not perfect – they are definitely far from what many back in Africa see as paradise. Granted, they may be better off than the majority of their brothers and sisters on the continent but we contend that Africans living in France are confronted with real challenges which must be solved – and by Africans ourselves.

Rigorous personal investment in thought and optimizing the utilization of time as a free resource is, in our view, still lamentably low among Africans in Europe even though the environment for conducting a different lifestyle is there. 'Can Africans think?' is a debate motion which should be discussed by each and every literate African in France. In fact, it is essentially over this thorny question that Senghor found himself seriously challenged by his African contemporaries who refused to answer 'no', like he seemed to confess. Yet on the basis of the results of many Africans' life style when they arrive in Europe (or France in particular), wouldn't the late poet's voice trouble our conscience? Have our tastes, actions and apparent dreams not tended to vindicate the objectionable statement by Senghor that we lack brain power compared to the indigenous inhabitants of Europe or France? Statistically, the numbers of high achievers among second generation

Africans in the diaspora must be closely examined. At the same time, the trend should also be understood as being indicative of the earlier generation's failure or success in achieving what they aimed at for their offspring. Ultimately, the military metaphor that, 'if you aim at nothing, you hit it' is starkly clear. It becomes a matter of asking what the Africans' precise aims, ambitions, targets – whether individually or as couples – for the children and finally collectively as aliens out here; daily, weekly, monthly, yearly, or per after every decade. The last part, at the level where 'thought' needs to be conducted – collectively as aliens, is of special importance and it is here where the impact of Africans in France can be prepared. 'Two heads are better than one' is a popular saying, yet few Africans try to consider the logical extension of this wisdom, i.e. if two heads are better than one, what if ten heads got together? Sadly, selfishness tends to become fashionable among Africans abroad, in a total reversal of Africans' past culture of human solidarity. If Africans can think, why is the aping of the Western world's often bizarre tastes, ways of thinking and non-values so widespread, let alone embarrassing?

Growing up in a former British colony, the author had the opportunity to know Africans on the continent in a national population that was multi-ethnic. There were Asians, Jews, Arabs and other foreigners like the English, Irish, French, Americans, Italians, etc. But in schools, we were taught and urged to consider affinities towards our closest kinds as inappropriate! It was referred to as tribalism. Certainly, speaking vernacular or one's mother tongue was punishable and derided. The reality in Europe is that their equivalent of tribes is regarded with esteem and preservation of the heritage of past societies such as the Bretons, Normans and so forth, is laudable. Why are Africans unable to revive this and begin to preserve our respective languages while we live out here? Must France take initiatives for Africans on this too? Well, if that was what Africans needed, here it is.

Africans should observe Asians, for example the Sri-Lankans or the different language groups who made up the 'boat-people', who lived in France a few decades ago. This applies to the Jewish people in this country as well. All the other people revere their cultural values, beliefs but above all, are very united in the way they protect their interests. If one Jew is touched, the entire local Jewish community becomes concerned. Vietnamese, Cambodians, and Sri-Lankans exist in networks. It seems these solidarity networks are what enable the weak ones to rise in strength. It is not uncommon to find six labourers living in s small studio, sharing very limited space and facilities. This may imply highly imaginative solutions such as having only three beds in such a place but ensuring that three of the occupants work at night while the other three work during day time!

There is also the strict discipline or honesty among these people; anyone in need borrows from those who have money. Cheating is abhorred and the culprit can be severely chastised by the rest of the group. One would wish Africans discovered these realities and organized themselves – to use them for collective improvement as a people. Sadly, the truth is that Africans tend to be unkind to one another when it comes to these matters of truthfulness, mutual assistance and general solidarity. Cheating the weak is rampant and success is mainly perceived as personal and being above the other(s). There is insensitivity to injustice done to another. Members of the community hardly come in as a factor to push in favour of the underprivileged ones. There appears to be a total negation of the idea that unity is strength among Africans in France. 'Divided we fall but together we stand' would be a motto for Africans in France to consider adopting. This is how those in competitive positions can count on support from fellow Africans because failure at one level means failure for all.

Conclusion

'Africans in France' is a tricky, instructive and particularly fascinating subject. France itself, from a historical viewpoint presents examples of some of the best men and women in terms of human qualities – thinkers, scientists, adventurers and military strategists that one can think of. At the same time, however, France has also produced individuals of unbelievable hardness of heart, insensitivity to other cultural values and inflexibility when confronted with seemingly insurmountable problems, whereas perhaps with a little flexibility one could find a solution to them. For those who may find this duality difficult to take in, the ancient French proverb, 'Il n'y a pas de roses sans épines' which means, 'There are no roses without thorns' might help.

As a nation, France is at least 2000 years old. Geographically, it has had bits and pieces of its territory across the oceans. At different epochs along its history, France has been overrun by alien invaders but has also in turn invaded other people and colonized them, in the West Indies, Africa and Asia. Some of the subjects from the colonies France created became French with time and today, even those who fought to become independent of France do return to France as immigrants staying in Metropolitan France. This discussion has endeavoured to provide a review of what the experiences of Africans in France, both overseas and in Europe, have been from the earliest people who entered France, all through the years until the present.

The earliest Africans to enter France came as invaders from northern Africa through Spain and imposed their rule for about four decades before they were routed by the valiant Galls in the 8th Century, AD. As part of the slave trading European nations, France participated in the trans-Atlantic slave trade and kept Africans as labourers on plantations in their West Indies colonies. Those Africans were in France and their experience is discussed. France later became fully involved in the European adventures to gain territorial control, do commerce and spread the Christian religion on the African continent. With France's colonial policy, its colonies constituted part of France so that the colonized people were Africans in France. Some colonies never became independent of France – leading to their continued occupation in France until today, for the Africans in those territories. The Africans in former French colonies which became independent just like any other African, may go on to and live in France today for a variety of reasons. All the above are the categories of people discussed in this chapter.

Conditions of Africans in France have also tremendously changed across the centuries. There have always been challenges for people from Africa, although it would be incorrect and unjust to charge that France has always been their source of suffering. Concrete cases are given where European French individuals fought in defence of the rights and dignity of Africans in France, to the point of paying with their own lives. Additionally, although it is generally claimed that the French authorities went out, enslaved or colonized Africans, cruelly treating them and trampling over their rights, it is clearly recorded that there were isolated occasions when the authorities in France dispatched military personnel to colonies in order to uphold the rule of law against European settlers' wishes in favour of the indigenous population. Evidence is given to show that France, like any other country, has divided views on many issues affecting Africans. This tends to follow the team of leaders in power at a given time. The 1789 revolution saw the application of its universal principles nullified by Napoleon Bonaparte in regard to Africans in France (on the island of Santo Domingo in the West Indies). The attitudes of some Africans themselves were, and continue to be, contributory factors in shaping what happens to Africans in France – abroad or in the Metropolis.

Africans in France today have a considerably favourable environment in which to thrive and must mainly blame themselves if they fail. France offers great opportunities for an African who has legitimately entered the country and lives here. As a result of the hard international economic situation coupled with the still lingering xenophobia on the part of warped minded people in France – like elsewhere in the world – conditions to get into the country have become increasingly tougher. It is true, therefore, that Africans already in France may face daily challenges in attaining their objectives. This can also be said for the native French as well. It is for the Africans in France to change the prevalent attitude of inferiority complex vis-à-vis Europeans and determinedly compete through resilience and sweat in order to prove that biologically, human beings differ only in what we choose to believe we are or aren't capable of.

On the whole, the French legal system provides every chance for any serious and honest African to reach their goal. Of course, in France (just like anywhere else), natives enjoy the most favourable legal status. Africans born in France are practically entitled to this. With hard work, perseverance and honest conduct anyone can apply and become French. Africans who want to see these conditions made even better must be role models to the young Africans in daily lifestyle. France appreciates and likes Africans who support its legitimate causes, who live in harmony with the republican ideals of liberty (with responsibility), equality and brotherhood. Some African brothers and sisters in the past did set laudable examples. Today, across the entire political ideological spectrum, men and women of African descent expect African aliens or naturalized ones to show appreciation, support and understanding for the efforts and even risks confronting them for the good of France and human rights. Africans in France cannot afford to slumber.

V

AFRICA'S EXTERNAL DEBT: AN UNAVOIDABLE NIGHTMARE?

"Why and how did almost every country in Africa borrow so much money when it did? Why is the external debt today, a rope round the neck of practically each nation that borrowed?"

'A fool and his money are soon parted.' - Thomas Tusser, Five Hundredth Pointes of Good Husbandrie, 1573[28].

Why and how did almost every country in Africa borrow so much money? Why is the external debt today, a rope around the neck of practically each nation that borrowed? These are not questions that appertain to rocket science, or require PhDs in economics to answer. The crux of the matter is that very little critical thought or open debate about the running of public affairs in Africa has been tolerated. Neither time nor thought are taken as crucial ingredients in the processes of governance. The absence of these two things make it possible for unethical tendencies fuelled by material greed, to undermine any objective analysis of issues confronting nations. Over time, the monster named corruption emerged and grew into the cancer that has crippled Africa economically, and continues to gnaw the continent to the bones.

'Borrowing' in African societies is commonly practiced as a normal short-term way of solving an urgent problem. This comes with a clear understanding that the means to repay, exists. Those who cannot guarantee pay back, out of self-respect, do not give empty promises. Such persons may simply be helped through alms or gifts.

However, this hasn't been the attitude with African politicians who decided to transact with money lenders from the West. It would be jumping to conclusions, if we said that the capitalists or former colonial powers once again victimized Africa by swindling her money in this way. To do so would be tantamount to once again assigning to African independent nations the

28 http://www.phrases.org.uk/meanings/a-fool-and-his-money-are-soon-parted. html

124

status of inferior, incompetent, and assisted entities masquerading as nations, without possessing the capacity to stand on their own feet. This discussion challenges Africans as nations, to stand up and speak to those they decide to partner with, as equals. This is what owning up and assuming accountability for actions or omissions boils down to. Independence must be precisely this or more, not less.

It is a well-established and known practice that with any financial institution in the West, raising a loan is not an easy matter. The borrower may, for instance, undertake a project to acquire a house or an apartment. Before approaching any lender, the borrower looks for an appropriate property. He collects as much information on the property as the bank requires him to assemble. When the property satisfies the bank as being worth the amount of money sought, the bank then sets out to literally strip the borrower naked. The person seeking the loan discloses his/her date of birth, health status, marital status, whether or not he/she has children and their exact ages, sex, etc. Then the bank demands information on the professional qualifications, present employment for both the borrower and his/her spouse, if married, and so forth. The bank also exhaustively carries out an investigation to establish, not just how much the potential borrower earns per month, but also the reliability of their employment contract or source of revenue. It is only after the bank is satisfied on all accounts, that it may commence negotiations with the borrower regarding the possibilities of lending him/her the money. It is at the end of this embarrassing ordeal that a loan may be granted, but the borrower must commit to surrendering all the property in question, should anything happen that prevents him from meeting the conditions stipulated in the agreement with the bank. This is why one talks of having a mortgage with the bank. All the above applies whether the deal involves only one hundred thousand dollars/euros, or millions of dollars/euros. Individuals, depending on the borrower's age, tend to ask for a repayment period of between 15-20 years, at a mutually agreed-upon interest rate.

It is against the above understanding of the stringent terms imposed by lenders on the one hand and the cautiousness involved on the other – implying a big sense of responsibility that the borrower enters into by taking a bank loan – that the subject of Africa's external debt has to be discussed. It should go without saying that a decision to borrow money – in this case huge sums of money – is arrived at in real concert, following thorough reflection and discussions where the borrower(s) are a couple or a nation. To unilaterally commit resources in this kind of way would be a sign of lunacy, if done without proper planning, and all concerned being in agreement.

To discuss Africa's external debt burden without seeking to simply exonerate lenders of the possible unfair schemes they may have concealed at the time of lending the money, and the fact that individual African countries had responsibilities to meet when they contracted the loans, must be clearly pointed out from the start.

In preparing themselves, it would be useful to know whether the legislature – the meeting place where people's representatives discuss and agree on their peoples' needs – freely and fully agreed on the amounts of money to be borrowed. Furthermore, if the answer to this question is in the affirmative, one would have to ascertain that qualified and objective professionals had the opportunity to examine the feasibility of the projects for which such a national debt should be contracted. If the projects were declared technically sound and feasible (besides their utility within the framework of national priority needs), then basic measures to minimize risks involved, can be said to have been taken.

It is this part that constitutes the bigger part of the borrowers' responsibility to prepare themselves. This is where foreseeable risks and expected benefits should have been analysed and made known to all. Parliaments will have approved the money to be borrowed while government (the executive) is only charged with ensuring that the technical aspects and the implications involved are thoroughly handled by the most able professionals. The entire process necessitated brains, transparency, patriotism, and ethics or moral rigor. What then, is the reality of the African external debt story?

Let us revisit the scenario; we have an individual borrower, who we shall call Mr X. Let that individual represent an African country that we shall call Y. This country (Y) borrows a sum of money to the tune of US$100 million from a foreign bank, on the basis that the bank is satisfied that Y can repay. In the event of failure to do so, there are assets that the bank can confiscate. In other words, some crucial national assets have been mortgaged. If the public debate and approval by the nation mentioned above duly took place, lenders would not push beyond this point as it would be on the verge of interfering in internal matters of a sovereign state.

In reality, however, the Executive arms of government in most African countries arrogated themselves the exclusive powers to borrow any amounts of money. The lenders, often with a hidden agenda, presented a façade of lenience to the borrowers. The latter, in characteristic opacity to doing government business, swallowed the poison. The role of objective trained professionals to critically examine the terms against which loans were being accorded was in most cases impossible, as political loyalty to those in power came first. Negotiators tended to be people that toed the political line – allowing greed complacency to undermine the professional discipline when confronted with commissions under the table.

This is where a question must be asked; why is it that all countries failed to safely meet their obligations towards their lenders? Naturally, the lenders had something up their sleeves in negotiating the loans they granted. But isn't this precisely why African people, governments and the leaders of the day in particular should tell the world how they played their roles in the negotiating process? Not every country had leaders like Bodel Bokassa, Idi Amin Dada, or Mobutu Sese Seko, who could be pardoned for lack of intellectual sophistication required to deal with the intricate issues which were involved here. Yet even in these extreme cases of incompetent heads of state, professionals were definitely involved. How does one possibly explain that countries went in for such long periods of debt repayment and in fact, eagerly welcomed these long periods, going up to as many as 10 years of 'grace'? Is it grace or stranglehold?

Did Africans truly scrutinize the 'period of grace' phrase that was so generously accorded to them as they borrowed the money? Is this not more evidence to suggest that for much of Africa, the understanding of 'time' and its implications needs to be improved? Is it unfair to say that had borrowers pondered more on it at that time, the ruin caused to the continent would have been averted or at the very least reduced? The British saying that "time is money" rings true here, because more years of grace meant more money for the lender – a fact Africans obliviously missed, as explained below.

No doubt, once the lenders identified securities in the countries lured into borrowing money, they avoided borrowers cross-examining them, to truly understand what they were going in for. Perhaps such measures might have 'awakened sleeping dogs' and thus the solidity or viability of projects for which loans were being sought, became less relevant. If anything, the lenders should have examined the project to ensure that it did not bear flaws that increased the chances of failure. At any rate, lenders were in pressing need to lend the money which depositors from OPEC states had placed with them, and were desperately hunting for borrowers who were not too meticulous in studying the terms given.

First of all, Africa must take the blame for naïvely taking the phrase 'grace period' at face value. The same African politicians had, for half a century, dealt with the hypocrisy of colonial and imperial businessmen. It is standard practice that banks expect interest to accrue on capital from the moment that money leaves their coffers and goes into the borrower's account. It becomes the borrower's responsibility to understand the implication of borrowing, US$1,000,000 for example, while suspending any repayments for a period of 10 years so that reimbursements commence in the eleventh year. All the interest that accrues over the decade cumulatively becomes capital lent to the borrower. Before demonstrating the ruinous consequences of this 'grace period' to Africa, one should be told why the countries accepted/sought this arrangement. In this context, ignorance is tantamount to blindness.

The trend of developments regarding the borrowed money, with focus on the heavy responsibility borne by the borrower is as follows: At an agreed fixed interest rate of 5%, US$1,000,000 is loaned with a grace period of 10 years. The actual time over which the loan is to be reimbursed could be anything from 10 to 30 years. The implications of this agreement for the two parties are totally dissimilar.

After year one, the interest which accrues on the capital of US$1,000,000 is US$50,000. For year two, the capital which the lender has becomes US$1,050,000. The interest on $1,050,000 for year two is US$52500. The capital for year three rises to US$1,102,500. In year four, the interest accrued on US$1,102,500 is US$55,125 leading to a capital of US$1,157,625 in year five. With this new figure for year five, the interest accrued in that year is US$57,881.25 making the capital for year six rise to US$1,215,506.25. Year six generates interest that amounts to US$60,775.31 bringing the lender's capital for year seven to US$1,276,282. Interest accrues in year seven to the tune of US$63,814.08 so that for year eight, the capital is 1,340,096. With this as capital, year eight brings an interest of US$67,005 leading to an increment in the capital for year nine to US$1,407.101. Year nine generates an interest of US$70,355 which results in a capital base of US$1,477,456. During year 10, the new capital accrues an interest of US$73,872 so that at the end of year 10, the borrower owes the bank US$1,551,329.

The reason why the borrowing state should have imperatively had a solid, viable and sustainable project in advance, is because when the money is received, the operations in the country where the money is to be used, needs to run at a profitability rate superior to the interest rate accruing in the bank, for the borrower to benefit from the loan. In this case, the minimum returns on investment per year at home ought to have been at least 7%.

Is there evidence that truly sound and sustainably executed projects existed in borrowing countries within Africa? It would have been impossible, if projects had been carefully designed in advance, for the debt to become ruinous to states. Another possibility is that the 'grace period' gimmick made borrowers relax until the eleventh year, when the process of repayment kicked off! However, by then it was too late to save the situation. The illustration above looks at a loan of only US$1,000,000 yet by the time repayments begun, the debt was over US$1,500,000. What about those countries that applied for hundreds of millions of dollars, yet their prior preparations for refund was flimsy? Time inevitably brought them down to their knees, and they would never to be able to economically rise up again. This happened because investing in thought, discipline, calculation, and objective judgment that form the basis of enlightened planning, was brushed aside. Leaders wanted to be told by those advising them only what they liked to hear, as opposed to what they needed to hear. On the other hand, the lenders concentrated on monitoring the time; months and years passed by as they diligently made sure that their carefully laid traps for the round-bellied African men fulfilled their purpose. The trick worked.

Other societies invest well in hard focused thought. The British bluntly declare, as stated above, that time is money. Many people in Africa have yet to take these point seriously. Meanwhile, misery and shame remain the distinguishing feature of the continent's people as a whole.

What has been described above may be compared to the story of a culturally blind fellow, who rents a limousine for a day from a crafty car rental company. He has a budget of only US$300 which he knows to be the daily fee for the impressive vehicle he needs to go out with a girl he wants to impress and eventually ask for her hand in marriage. Being Muslim, he picks the vehicle on Thursday after work since he will be off duty on Friday. On Friday evening, he uses the vehicle with his girlfriend and then drives to the company to return the car on Saturday morning. However, he finds the place closed and later learns that the business is run by a Seventh-day-Adventist. The following day is Sunday, Easter Sunday to be exact, which makes the day after a public holiday i.e. Easter Monday. In a predominantly Christian country, that is not a working day either! The poor man, having not considered local customs ends up with a three-day extra bill to pay. On the contract he signed that Thursday, the warning in small letters at the bottom stated that 'clients must pay a 50-dollar surcharge for every 24 hours of delay in returning a vehicle'. Of course like most people, he hadn't read the fine print and on Tuesday, the company presents him with a bill of US$450 bill instead of the US$300 he expected! That wasn't the worst that happened to the man that weekend, though. His focus had been more on the beauty he was hiring the limousine for – an obsession that made him so absent minded. Trouble began when the girl did not turn up that Friday night claiming to be out of town with her family in the village for the Easter festivities. In all his planning, he had not ascertained the lover's presence that Friday evening. And as there was no phone service in the village where the girl went, the two only spoke on Monday afternoon after she had returned to town, exhausted and unable to go out until the following Friday!

Similar to the above, the fluid nature of African country projects, for which large sums of money were borrowed, is partly the rationale for the countries' failures to create profits from borrowed capital. Insufficient analysis of the reasons for which money was borrowed cannot be blamed on the lenders entirely. For lenders, making profit on the capital lent out, is their principle objective or major concern. It is the responsibility of those who take out the loan to safeguard their own interest. This ability to safeguard Africans' own economic interest is what was inadequate. To realize this and admit that Africa itself is largely responsible for the sorry economic conditions of its people, is the only condition for emancipation.

One may ask, 'Why do Africans put the blame on others, even today?' There are numerous possible answers to this question. Firstly, the misconception that lenders are simply generous – thus the expectation that ethical virtues guide commercial transactions.

Secondly, the inability to recognize when our behaviour and conduct run against declared objectives. Thirdly, sheer ineptitude in handling complexities involved in present day international affairs, and more.

The first – believing in lenders' generosity – is as true as saying that Africans suffer from an acute dependency syndrome. It is this mental malady that predisposes whole presidents and ministers to go hat-in-hand abroad, looking for budget subsidies. Self-respect is the first casualty in this exercise which leaves 'donors' giggling, and embolden them to shamelessly dictate terms to Africans. In 2012 the British Prime Minister David Cameron, openly declared that Africans must either accept the promotion of marriage between people of the same sex in their societies, or risk having no financial assistance! In today's state of intercultural intelligence, this was like a situation where the French who normally eat horse meat and frog legs might tell the British to start eating the same, or risk losing mutual trading exchanges. The British are a great and proud people who would not suddenly revise culinary traditions they've had for centuries. The French traditionally frown at the apparent love the British have for the popular fish and chips staple, yet this has not caused the English to abandon this favoured dish. Differences in cultural practices should be respected.

Why should anybody make the kind of statement Mr Cameron made in the field of cooperation? Fortunately, not all the British people have this attitude toward the rest of the world. Otherwise it would have been necessary, for all self-respecting political leaders in Africa to state in unison that Mr Cameron and those like him keep their money until such a time when they can do business based on mutual respect.

Respect – particularly self-respect – is the very basis of the African concept 'Ubuntu'; that which makes one a human. A self-respecting beggar will throw back the coin to a giver, who spits in his face as he gives it to him. Givers of alms should strictly conduct themselves in ways that reflect recognition of the recipient as a fellow human being. Inferiority complex, which in turn breeds the inferiority syndrome, stands as one of the central problems Africans must combat. Former South Africa's President, Thabo Mbeki's CARS[29] will significantly contribute to Africa's rebirth if this is considered one of its central missions.

Even if a situation of "zero" external interference was obtained, Africa's serious internal problems would still have made reimbursing borrowed money very difficult. Uganda in East Africa, and Liberia in West Africa, are two cases which, on close examination, show this paradox.

The popular theme of the millennium development goals (MDGs) lends itself handy in illustrating the intricacy of declared objectives and the realities on the ground. Liberia shows this contradiction most poignantly.

First of all, even assuming that when African countries borrowed money during the '70s, Liberia had well thought out investment projects for which to take loans, Liberians had a heavier responsibility – to guarantee the money's profitable utilization over the agreed period, once the money was in their possession, in order for the country to benefit from it while at the

---

29 "CARS" stands for Centre for African Renaissance Studies.

same time ensuring repayments according to schedule. It is going to be shown that it takes more than technically sound projects to meet debt obligations.

In 1980, a coup d'état took place in Liberia, leading to the assassination of President William Tolbert and the public extra-judicial execution of many members of his government. The years which followed were politically volatile, culminating in the 1990 gruesome assassination of President Samuel Kanyon Doe. Political instability turned into civil war well before the ousting of Samuel Doe, and went on for 14 years under President Charles Taylor until he was pressured into stepping down in order for a transitional government to be formed, under the chairmanship of Mr Gyude Bryant in 2003.

Politicians' responsibility to consciously conduct affairs of their country in a manner that ensures the nation's ability to fulfil obligations vis-à-vis its creditors, was seriously lacking. For the creditors, however, the contractual conditions weren't waived. Therefore, the interest on the capital borrowed, continued to accrue over all this period. Leaders in many countries dodged the real issues, while they squandered the available resources. The Liberian case seems to illustrate this point in terms of how Africans themselves can ruin a healthy and promising economy. Liberians admit that from 1982 the effects of political leadership with limited capacity to run the country, resulted in the deepening of the nation's indebtedness. The total external debt stock of the country had risen from US$726 million (or 75 per cent of GDP) in 1982, to US$1.8 billion (or 164 per cent of GDP) in 1988, with the debt-service payments shooting up from US$45 million (9 per cent of export earnings) to US$197 million (40 per cent of export earnings) over the same period. (Geepu Nah Tiepoh, *The Human and Economic Plight of a Nation,* The Perspective, May 4, 2001).

The same analyst of his country's external debt imbroglio states that in 1990, Charles Taylor at the head of a military junta, took power on the day of Samuel Doe's assassination. An enlightened group of Liberians assumed political leadership, albeit undemocratically. The new politicians paid very little attention to the country's external debt obligations. The successive governments from 1990 virtually abandoned debt-service payments, and arrears fast accumulated. The country virtually ignored the debt problem. This led Liberia's external public debt to astronomically rise to US$2.6 billion by the end of 1999, and further to US$3.5 billion by 2001.

It has also been legitimately argued by analysts, that Africa's external debt problems aren't entirely caused by factors endogenous to the continent. Nevertheless, the analysts do concede that 'imprudent debt management policies by borrowing countries, and use of loans on projects of doubtful viability… undermined the capacity of countries to repay loans…' (Debt Sustainability: Oasis or Mirage? In ECONOMIC DEVELOPMENT IN AFRICA, United Nations Conference on Trade and Development, 2004, pp8.). The fact that political change in Africa almost invariably came about through the barrel of the gun – preceded and followed by grave civil strife lasting for years – prevented countries from concentrating on economic activities, which therefore undermined repayments.

The environment created by a nasty civil war, is hard to imagine for one hasn't lived through it or worked in the throes left behind. We lived through the immediate post war conditions in Uganda, Haiti, Rwanda and Liberia. The Liberian and Sierra Leone context are a case apart in that they each lasted for over a decade, and their overall impact on the populations – beyond the level of savagery on the civilians – resulted in turning every person into an IDP[30]. The able-bodied travelled hundreds of miles to escape the killings and maiming. Women suffered most; they were raped, tortured or captured, and held as sex slaves by the fighters when they weren't killed. In Liberia, it was doubly dangerous to be a woman and pregnant. The elderly and very young were either killed or forced into fighting as child soldiers.

Economic activity like growing crops was nil. Survival was the daily focus for many, for 14 years in Liberia. It is not that one wants to be disrespectful, but those who even remotely share responsibility in igniting such conditions in a country should be made to publicly repent. Economically, unfortunately, it was those same people who diverted the little national resources available, to the purchase of weapons. Those weapons, after being used to slaughter their compatriots, ended up being directed against neighbouring populations, like was the case when Charles Taylor's mercenaries took it upon themselves to destabilize Guinea and Sierra Leone. Within the context of African economic development, it becomes clear that leaders' ineptitude in managing the affairs of their people, spelt doom.

---

30 IDP stands for Internally Displaced Person(s).

The problem is a lot more complex than it appears, for a number of reasons. There are only a few objective and frank professionals who will speak candidly to Africans. African politicians seem to be extremely intolerant to criticism. Nationals who try to do so either end up marked for no promotion if employed in state institutions, or are falsely accused for being traitorous, if they are not forced into fleeing to distant lands as political asylum seekers. This deprives most countries of the very brains needed to prevent the deepening of foreign debts. It is part of the art that foreign advisors master; remaining politically correct in what they tell the people in power. While some of them do perform a valuable job, many have interests that aren't compatible with the national ones. Susan George bluntly sates that '…heavy dependence on foreign agencies for technical assistance is a natural corollary to the unwillingness of leaders to squarely face the basic problems of the country.' (Susan George, How the Other Half Dies, pp40.)

Susan George in 1977, conveyed Frantz Fanon's indignation about the conduct of Africa's elite by reproducing his words that the 'national middle class ought to consider as its bounden duty to put at the people's disposal, the intellectual and technical capital it has snatched when going through the colonial universities…' adding that in reality these elites have betrayed every hope placed in them. Susan George continues the citation: 'Intellectual laziness, spiritual penury, cowardice at the decisive moment,' she says, 'are some of the milder charges Fanon levels at Under Developed Countries middle class.' For Susan, Fanon found in the African Elite most of the nastier traits of the colonialists, plus some of their own '…narcissistic, completely ignorant of the economy of their own country, stupid, contemptibly, cynically bourgeois.' (Susan George, How the Other Half Dies, The real reasons for World Hunger, 1977, Local Elites- pp. 63.)

Fundamentally, the whole debate over the external debt in Africa has gone on for far too long. If it were a simple matter of brains, the staff of the World Bank, the International Monetary Fund, the African Development Bank and others, should have found the remedy by now. They will not, however, because the cancer has now spread all over the continent's bodies. The solution lay in Africa fully understanding the game it was enticed into, prior to engaging. The second part of the medicine should have been that money borrowed under the terms laid before governments, should have been injected into projects with all seriousness, rigor and an acute sense of accountability based on awareness of time. To meet such conditions, rulers should have relaxed their grip on power so that confrontations, wars, dissidents and other avoidable political squabbles are averted. Patriotism should have dictated good governance to create environments where economic activities and investment, as well as tourism, are to prosper. All these are issues people in a country can put in place if they weigh the negative consequences such as the current foreign debt overhang against what peace brings.

Africa is economically bleeding, and will continue to do so even after paying back what is received from creditors:

'A cursory glance at Africa's debt profile shows that the continent received some $540 billion in

loans and paid back some $550 billion in principal and interest between 1970 and 2002. Yet Africa remained with a debt stock of $295 billion. For its part, south of the Sahara Africa (SSA) received $294 billion in disbursements and paid $268 billion in debt service, but remains with a debt stock of some $210 billion.'

Figure 1: The genesis and nature of the external debt in Africa, (page 8, African Debt Crisis.)

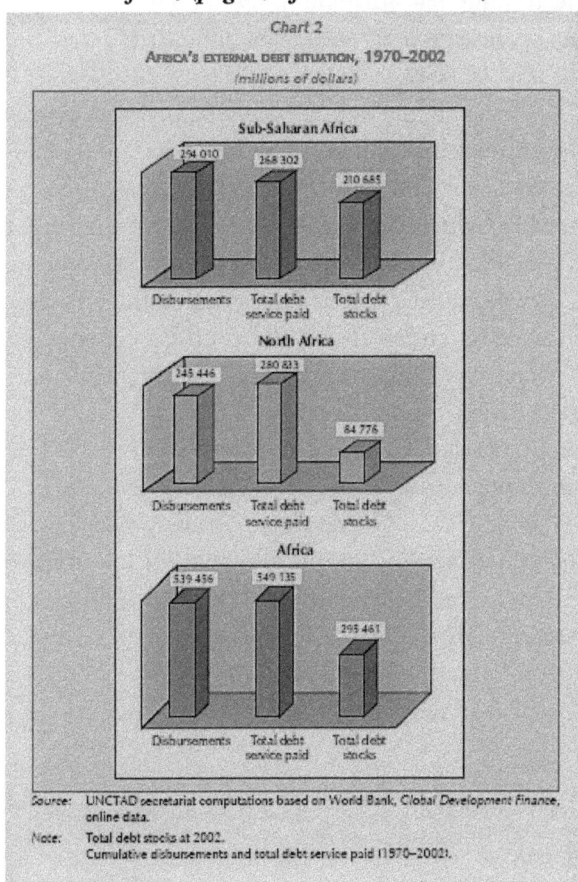

Chart 2

AFRICA'S EXTERNAL DEBT SITUATION, 1970–2002
(millions of dollars)

Source: UNCTAD secretariat computations based on World Bank, Global Development Finance, online data.

Note: Total debt stocks at 2002.
Cumulative disbursements and total debt service paid (1970–2002).

The last word hasn't been said on Africa's 'incurable' economic suicide. It is indeed in this sense of 'suicide' that Africa herself has the power, the key, and the solution to this self-inflicted cancer of the external debt overhang. If Africa can determine her death, albeit perhaps inadvertently, why shouldn't she be able to extricate herself from it? This is precisely where 'thought' becomes the critical issue. Can Africans pool together all necessary resources and figure out how to end this infernal situation? There is no reason to think that because for fifty years Africa didn't solve a problem, it is impossible to solve it now.

Although the Idi Amin persona became a famous caricature of African leadership for his seeming lack of knowledge or diplomatic *finesse*, the actions of the so-called 'enlightened' did not make much of a difference in Uganda. Infuriated by the facts about the economic suicide Ugandans and Liberians committed through engaging in fratricidal civil wars for decades during the '80s and '90s, we established a constant key feature. The heaviest economic nose-down occurred with the height of war. Conversely, the economy picked up almost phenomenally as a space of peace returned.

Kwame Nkrumah's admonition and Thabo Mbeki's recommendations31 return resounding as guiding principles to self-respect and autonomy32.

---

31 "I represent a people who know the benefits of **the dividend of peace**, who look forward to a life free of poverty and underdevelopment.... You have come here to give practical expression to the dream of millions of Africans,..."
32 Source - http://afrolegends.com/2012/10/02/kwame-nkrumah-first-president-of-ghana/("Seek ye first the political kingdom, and all else shall be added unto you") and ; The peace Dividend

"I represent a people who know the benefits of the dividend of peace, who look forward to a life free of poverty and underdevelopment ..." Thabo Mbeki – 20 03.

"Seek ye first the political kingdom, and all else shall be added unto you." Kwame Nkrumah – 1957

Uganda's Political Experience and Its External Debt Crashing Burden

From January 1971 to April 1979, Uganda was to be run by Idi Amin Dada's military junta. In Africa, it is normal to attribute any such coup d'état to some foreign interference. Not that one can entirely dismiss all extraneous factors. What is critical here, just like was the case in the genesis of the external debts, there is a good possibility that the people in government at that time probably created for themselves the conditions for the ultimate collapse of the Obote I government in Uganda. Focusing here on the element 'thought' and 'time', would it be too far-fetched to say that internal disquiet, disagreements, intrigues, betrayal and fear out of mutual suspicion got to such high – in fact explosive levels within the ruling camp itself that 'things fell apart'? Uganda's political evolution, focusing particularly on citizens themselves, whatever the truth was, by and large, Mr Milton Obote's fall did not come as a big surprise to many. It can be said without fear of contradiction, that Idi Amin's arrival in office met with very little, if any mass protest in Uganda. In fact, in many parts of the country people publicly celebrated in streets.

With hindsight one sees the highly qualified personalities who made up Mr Obote's first government. Yet, all their academic/professional credentials did not stop them from letting democratic institutions run down, or from collapsing the justice system with all the safeguards of people's human rights withering away. Was it then the illiterate man put at the helm of the state system who was going to stop this huge downward spiral of ethics? Perhaps. Some dared to hope while others despaired!

Idi Amin turned up with a team of cabinet ministers which may have been the most highly qualified on the continent, all countries considered at the time. This was to be short lived, however, as within less than two years there were numerous changes regarding ministers and their posts.

Idi Amin's government inherited the state system in the form Mr Milton Obote's year of tinkering left it. The fundamental questions which a genuinely non-sectarian political leader had to address had remained unaddressed in earnest, since independence. Forging the nation was on politicians' lips but truly concrete sustainable action strategies were hardly embarked on. Instead, towards the end of his nine years in power, Idi Amin's predecessor had come to rely more and more on the military to safeguard his own position. Idi Amin thus arrived fully aware of the fact that political power lay with the army in Uganda. During the eight years he stayed in power he in turn relied on the military for practically everything he did in office.

While democratic government institutions suffered atrophy under Milton Obote – Parliament becoming a rubber stamp, the judiciary observing only 'politically correct' aspects of the law, and the Executive becoming not accountable except for the appointing political powers – Idi Amin banned any political activities all together. Parliament was closed, the fate of the Judiciary was symbolized by the broad-day dragging of the Chief Justice from the High Court building and his mysterious murder that followed. Justice came under perpetual threat. As for the Executive powers of government under Idi Amin, it became hard to tell whether things improved on what existed under Milton Obote or deteriorated.

The departure of the colonial administration was firmly justified as necessary in order for nationals to run the country themselves. In hindsight, the colonial administration deserved credit for putting in place strong and credible, functioning institutions. Practically every sector of public life was effectively run, and met the needs of Ugandans throughout the territory – with the exception of resistant Karamoja. The Obote group of national office holders inherited the system that was literally in 'perfect' working order. Regrettably, inefficiency started creeping into state institutions once the strict discipline formerly kept by the British in regard to screening during recruitment, the unbiased selection of successful candidates, and the fair play in management (rewards and reprimands being given where and as due), began to drop. Partisan considerations in recruitment, promotion, etc., with political consideration, increasingly became the determining factor.

By the time Idi Amin burst onto the scene, nine years from the time the British left, some things had changed beyond recognition, very often for the worse. Within the national army where Idi Amin was, it had been well known that he had enjoyed special and accelerated promotion by President Milton Obote, out of the personal trust and close relationship they had with each other. Idi Amin most probably knew that he wasn't the most qualified for the high rank he held in the army if strictly professional criteria had been adhered to. The same incomprehension surrounded Mr Obote's decision to promote another junior soldier – Smith Opon-Acak when he returned to office over a decade later.

In this respect, Idi Amin could be regarded as a leader who copied his methods from his boss. If Mr. Milton Obote noticeably diminished the independence and efficient functioning of state institutions – the case of the legislative body and the military have been explained - Idi Amin exacerbated the problem by either staffing them with friends and confidants that in some instances could hardly read or write, or simply disregarded the institutions all together. This became particularly evident with the top appointments in the Army, Ministry of Foreign Affairs and within Police Service.

Disregard for professional or academic qualifications in appointments to public offices, had devastating consequences on Uganda's development. State institutional performance dropped, while the waste of valuable resources continued. Able citizens within institutions became demoralized or sought better professional challenges, either elsewhere in the country or abroad. The political environment in some ways started to resemble that of Mr Milton Obote's time, causing a considerable number of people with differing views, to flee the country.

Uganda, for almost two decades after independence, was a country where those running the state marginalized merit, and promoted 'yes men' that were ready to trade ethical principles for favours. Opportunism and short-termism in the pursuit of political and economic gains, emerged. It is in turn these dimensions of the subculture that bred rampant corruption that afflicts society to this day, regrettably mostly in high places. In these conditions, 'thought' was blunted while 'time', was wasted like squandered money. Issues which required hard cogitation in order to be sorted out, were not addressed. Succeeding generations end up having to confront the same problem because earlier on, Ugandans dedicated little or no time to think about them. Engrossed in squabbles over what could be easily analysed with sobriety, some natural resources that would earn the nation wealth from abroad are left to waste and even disappear. Two examples show this ineptitude with Ugandans.

The 1980 elections were considered neither transparent nor fair by a good part of Ugandans. The judicial system in Uganda, as pointed out above, had often been the victim of political influences. It failed, at moments of critical need, to serve as the neutral arbiter. Many scholars have expressed the view that those elections were rigged in favour of one political party which had the means to have its way. That dispute, which under a normal functioning judicial system could have been adjudicated through courts, ended in those objecting to the verdict taking up arms to militarily challenge the establishment. This turned out to be a protracted five-year liberation war. The debate as to whether or not war should have been waged is not the issue here. What is significant is that the economy of the country suffered a terrible blow which neither those in government nor the National Resistance Movement (NRM) intended. The explanation, however, is simple:

In Uganda in 1962, tourism ranked as the country's third most important foreign exchange earner, with wild game and natural geographical features as the leading attractions for visitors. Although ranked 10th in the world for possessing the most diversified range of mammalian species today, Uganda has not ably protected its animal population with the passing of time.

Other nations elsewhere, with comparable challenges, have worked out solutions. In fact, some nations such as Switzerland and Singapore, created artificial tourist attractions which enable them to earn even more revenue.

What happened in Uganda brings out the central missing ingredients for many countries in Africa but which, if the notions of reasonableness and elite accommodation as well as consociation of the national project are kept in view, would avoid conflict. Some analysts have boldly come out to urge our leaders to respect ethics – accept accountability, strengthen truthfulness, fight greed and selfishness. Systems like the Swiss come from ancient times – the 13th Century, but they had to start from somewhere.

African countries should practice legitimate leadership rotations from all regions of the country. Once again, Uganda is a country whose recent past history would have been easily helped by this approach. There were four well defined regions or provinces at the time of independence. Ugandans would be reasonably satisfied with constitutional arrangements that would give a turn to every region to raise the head of state – say after every five years. If that had been thought of, Sir Edward Mutesa for instance, should have only stayed in office for the first five years and left another leader from outside Buganda to hold the office in the country. This way, nobody from the central province would have come to lead Uganda before 1977. Rotation, as the Swiss have done it, reduces the feeling of alienation in parts of society. Stability reigns and the peace dividend – economic growth ensues and so does scientific work.

Occasionally, it may become necessary to defend a prolonged tenure of office by a given individual as is the case of, for example, Singapore's Lee Kuan Yew, Cuba's Fidel Castro, and Tanzania's first President Julius Nyerere. In reality, if the external threat may be too great, like the case of Cuba, then there is justifiable continuity. Otherwise, there is much that can be said in favour of the Swiss rotational arrangement.

Africa would have to emulate something else which we see to be of extreme importance: this is the primacy of institutions and norms. The state is a system, just like a clock. It ticks away and everyone allows it to function. Collective life must be allowed to run as smoothly as the rhythm of day and night. This is not only for the presidents to strictly observe, but also dutifully ensure that it works. The police, public transport operators, train services, postal staff as well as the hospitals, must operate within this logic.

It is the health and strong discipline at the level of government that leads the private sector to serve society satisfactorily because any deviation from what the law says is justly sanctioned. It then becomes very difficult for unscrupulous characters to abuse the innocent law-abiding citizens. The scene just described sounds like a mystic paradise, yet this is what we have observed in Switzerland. There is no mystery about it; the state/government and society are mutually reinforcing. This is what development ought to mean in Africa. It is striking that the explanation of Africa's economic growth exception and miracle sounds like this too[33]. Countries in Europe on the whole, approach perfection in this manner, and systems work quite well.

For nearly forty years, Jean-Jacques Rousseau was our favourite political philosopher as the father of 'guided democracy'. All along we thought, like many

33 State and private predation have been quite limited. Despite the large revenues from diamonds, this has not induced domestic political instability or conflict for control of this resource. The government sustained the minimal public service structure that it inherited from the British and developed it into a meritocratic, relative-ly non-corrupt and efficient bureaucracy, An African Success Story: Botswana paper by Daron Acemoglu, Simon Johnson and James A. Robinson July 11, 2001-(http://www.colby.edu/economics/faculty/jmlong/ec479/AJR. pdf) Respect for institutions – even the pre-colonial ones in Botswana: Our conjecture is that Botswana's institutions reflect a combination of factors. These include tribal institutions that encouraged broad based participation and constraints onpolitical leaders during the pre-colonial period; only limited effect of British colonization onthese pre-colonial institutions because of the peripheral nature of Botswana to the BritishEmpire; the fact that upon independence, the most important rural interests, chiefs and cattleowners, were politically powerful; the income from diamonds, which generated enough rentsfor the main political actors that it increased the opportunity cost of further rent seeking; andfinally, a number of important and farsighted decisions by the post-independence politicalleaders, in particular SeretseKhama and QuettMasire.(pp4)

people, that he was one of the most enlightened French thinkers. Research revealed he was not French. Jean-Jacques Rousseau was actually a Geneva-born Swiss. One finds very many profound philosophical principles which guide human life in Switzerland, even today. One could say that authority enforces the application of the golden rule. At this point, the philosophy instituted by Mr Lee Kuan Yew in Singapore in the '60s, transformed a country that very much resembled countries in Africa in many ways, into a leading world economic power today. Lee Kuan Yew too insists on an ethical society based on solid moral obligations. This has been translated into a culture of accommodation, guided by firm personal and collective discipline for the upholding of the rule of law.

If African countries recognized the 'peace dividend' as illustrated in the cases of Switzerland and Singapore, and did everything to avoid wars which have cost them so many human lives as well as economic growth over the last 50 years, it would have brought Africa comparable peace and development. This would imply that critical thought, integrity and foresighted political ambitions, should be made the basis of all forms of leadership. Mercifully, at least one of the African Union's 50 or so member states, provides key proof that failure is not a fatality for Africa.[34]

The distinctive work by three scholars on the Republic of Botswana in 2001 under the title *An African Success Story: Botswana* comes as a tiny flicker of hope in an otherwise totally obscure, bad situation. Looking at the story of Botswana from its time of independence

34 As of January 18 January 2014, Egypt, Madagascar, Guinea Bissao and the Central African Republic were under suspension for various reason. (http://en.wikipedia.org/wiki/African_Union#Membership).

in 1966, Daron Acemoglu, Simon Johnson and James A. Robinson stun the world with the following two opening sentences to their paper's abstract:

> 'Botswana has had the highest rate of per-capita growth of any country in the world in the last 35 years. This occurred despite adverse initial conditions, including minimal investment during the colonial period and high inequality'[35].

The above positive assertions, which are less than two decades old, carry a similar tone to an observation made about Africans by Lord Hailey in his monumental work titled *An African Survey*, undertaken in the year 1933. He, too, must have astounded the world when he wrote that:

> '...in 1932-34 two members of the Kenya Medical Service published a certain comparison between the brains of Europeans and Africans, in which one compared their cranial capacity and the other the characteristics of the cells of the pre-frontal cortex. The results were accepted in some quarters as evidence of the inferior mental capacity of the African, but recent studies of the brain have failed to establish any correlation between cranial capacity and mental intelligence...it is noteworthy in this particular connexion that Eskimo,

35 An African Success Story: Botswana paper by Daron Acemoglu, Simon Johnson and James A. Robinson July 11, 2001-(http://www.colby.edu/economics/faculty/jmlong/ec479/AJR.pdf)

Javanese and some Bantu tribes return higher averages of cranial capacity than the French or English...'[36]

The reader, if he/she is an African, may have thought all is lost to this continent and been tempted to give up the fight for self-esteem. But it is never too late.

While it is true that much time was lost, the future is intact and will be what current Africans and their supporters or friends decidedly labour to make it. 'Impossible' is a word to drop from our vocabulary as Africans. Africans are created and born just as other humans – if the Universal Declaration of Human Rights as propagated by the world's people i.e. the United Nations in 1948, is to be belie

---

36 Lord Hayley in An African Survey 1956 edition - see CHAPTER II - The African Peoples – Physical and mental Characteristics- the Cranial Index – pp44

VI

ON GENDER ISSUES IN AFRICA

Womanhood, Africa's Misery Trap

Gender is one area of query which still attracts very little critical reflection among African thinkers, cultural activists, political leaders or artists at home and in the Diaspora. Although this is and has been so for a long time, this chapter posits that the subject is central to Africa's ultimate veritable emancipation, economic self-sustenance, cultural self-realization and dignity. In parallel, the argument is presented that the ensuing misery afflicting Africans is largely of Africans' own creation and is avoidable.

Gender issues in Africa's experience as a subject may not strike many in and outside the African continent as a pivotal and burning issue that all Africans ought to wrestle with and sort out to ensure survival as a people. Quite often, there is even confusion between the terms 'gender' and 'sex'. This chapter will, first of all, establish a clear distinction between the two labels. After that, we shall look at the two closely related concepts of woman and man, which in this context are the 'gender labels' as opposed to the scientific categorization of human beings into the female and male kinds based on sex.

In addition to the main concepts of womanhood and manhood, the word 'misery' in the title of the paper will be explained as well as the reasons why it was chosen instead of any other comparable term. The term misery is used here because of its multi-dimensional attributes that accurately convey the image of the condition in which many ordinary Africans, particularly the rural women, live today. What constitutes womanhood, and what exactly is misery for African people? What is the nexus between men's attitude towards women and Africa's misery and Sub-Saharan Africa's failure to extricate itself from this condition for now over half a century?

"Aren't 'male dominance' and misery linked?"

The scope of this chapter has been deliberately condensed to specifically use few but very concrete local references. It first focuses on Uganda, where three societies whose traditional attitudes and practices regarding gender are remarkably familiar. Despite this narrow base, however, benefiting from the fortuitous access gained on other African cultural practices in other countries, a number of gender-related cases will also be cited from Western and Southern Africa. With this wider, though less specific geographical coverage, it is hoped that the cases used will reasonably represent Africans' attitudes on gender in general – 'womanhood' and 'manhood' – from Dakar to Mogadishu and from Cairo to Cape Town. Reference to cultural material from other cultures in the world will also be made.

Definitions

1. *Biology and sociology: sex and gender*

The moment a child is born in Africa, its biological sexual class is unmistakably identified. The child arrives as either female or male. Society, particularly the parents, start accompanying the child through infancy, childhood, puberty, teen age years and ultimately to the corresponding social status of woman or man. In other words, these are labels that are culturally constructed and assigned in contrast to the first two biological descriptive categories in which human beings fall by birth.

In most African cultural practices, a person's mere possession of the external male tool for procreation does not necessarily qualify the owner to bear the title 'man'. A male person of advanced age could be referred to as not being a man, or even more openly, he may be described as a woman. This is an infuriating insult that could result in the offended party staging a fight as proof of his manliness or manhood. On the contrary, if a woman is described as possessing manly traits, it is considered a compliment in most African societies. However, this is quite rare.

A tradition in the *Bagisu* society requires every male child at about 15 years of age to undergo an initiation rite into manhood – a physical and public circumcision ordeal. No form of anaesthesia is permitted as the subject concerned is required to show his capacity to stand the very acute pain without flinching. This form of initiation of individuals into manhood is rare in Uganda and East Africa in general, although quite a number of societies in Central Kenya, for example, the Kikuyu on the lower slopes of Mount Kenya, practised it at the time Jomo Kenyatta was growing up. In most West African societies, however, practically every male child is made to go through a whole series of instructions which culminate in the cutting. Those who are familiar with the Liberian traditions will recognize the terms *Poro* and *Sande* society schools.

On the other hand, while the males in Buganda culture do not undergo any form of physical pain in public, the notion of manhood carries even more significance in daily life. Here, the ultimate reference symbol of manhood is the *Kabaka* (King), who is in fact referred to as the husband of men, *Sabasajja,* i.e.

the 'number one man'. Among the Baganda, every mature male is automatically regarded as a man except in the few cases where an individual is publicly found to be sexually impotent, markedly cowardly, too lazy to do any work or henpecked. Even then, an individual who is generally considered to have the above social drawbacks is not to be ordinarily referred to as a woman. This only happens when and where such a person breaks an accepted rule of behaviour or annoys another person. It is only then that an offended member of society, who could even be a woman herself, may challenge the insolent individual to show his manhood! For example, one such challenge may be, "You are a woman!" Feuds used to start from this kind of utterance before the advent of modern mechanisms of settling disputes. What is implied here is that to be considered a woman among African men is to be degraded.

It is interesting to note that the King's daughters were addressed as men in the Baganda culture – "Ssebo i.e. Sir"! Moreover, a princess chose the man she wanted for a husband – without the man in question having the right to say no. It is probably this gender requirement that explains why President Idi Amin Dada, visiting as the new Ugandan Head of State at a state banquet hosted by Her Majesty Queen Elizabeth II of Britain in London, is said to have respectfully addressed the British female monarch as "Sir, Mr Queen..." Idi Amin was religiously adhering to the Buganda princely etiquette norms!

The *Iteso* (or Teso), the third society from Uganda, is chosen for their particular attitude towards a woman whose husband has died. While the Sati in traditional Indian culture went to the extreme extent of having the widow burn during the cremation of the dead husband, and some Nigerian societies believed in making the widow drink the water used to wash the dead husband's corpse, an Etesot widow undergoes such serious objectification that her status as a person is reduced to the husband's family property. The treatment negates most of her fundamental human rights. First of all, a widow becomes the wife of the heir to the deceased husband or his brother. Iteso widowers remain free to remarry according to their own choice. The imposed husband inherits the widow in very much the way he takes ownership of the rest of the deceased relative's property, i.e. house, cows etc. This is doubly infuriating where the widow happens to be a self-respecting person for whom a polygamous marriage is not an option. Considered from the health and legal standpoints, this takes us into the realms of vulnerability to all kinds of diseases, including HIV/AIDS and institutionalized rape. The inheritor assumes his deceased father's or brother's conjugal responsibilities regarding all the widows except his natural mother. Not that there couldn't be advantages to this social arrangement. The question is about the level of mutual respect and freedom of expression, free choice of a sexual partner and the quality of balanced rearing for each child in this setting from a father who may have three wives or more.

The above information shows men's general attitude towards women. Men are obsessed with male superiority over women. They constantly act to prove their manhood or absolute power and authority. This is sometimes carried out in extremely dangerous ways. How the Maasai of Kenya does this makes the *Imbalu* of the Bagisu look like child's play. Maasai young males are said to be subjected not only to circumcision as mentioned above but are also required to actually participate in solo or group lion hunting expeditions where they must kill the beast. Traditionally, the hunters are only armed with a spear and a stick. Those who know about the fierceness and power of a lion in its natural habitat would consider this utter craziness, but the Maasai men practice the rituals.

Men's inclination to prove their abilities and superiority over women takes some blood-chilling forms of public display outside the African continent. The rituals practiced by the Nangol (Vanuatu Land Divers) – the inhabitants of the Pentecost Island in the Pacific Ocean deserve special mention.

It is against the above forms of males' efforts to prove 'manhood' – toughness, courage, high risk-taking capacity, and enduring physical pain, that the discussion now turns to what remains as the content of 'womanhood' in Africa for both men and women.

Culturally, men have successfully put it in everyone's head that being a 'man' or attaining manhood is a positive superior state while being a woman is automatically seen as negative. In other words, the label woman almost always places a human being at a lower status. This is not a light generalization of our attitudes. We know from our experience as children and on the basis of observation throughout our lives so far that the treatment reserved for female human beings in everyday life is unenviable. For instance, in Buganda, girls and women traditionally must kneel to greet male members of society. The only exception is where the man being greeted is a pauper or without any social standing. This form of 'showing respect' is not expected of even little male children, regardless of the importance of a female person being saluted. Interestingly, men prostrate themselves to the ground while saluting the monarch, the lion (*Mpologoma*).

2. *Misery*

Traditionally, an African is a very proud person. In this regard, culturally, the sense of personal dignity cannot be said to be different whether the person is a man or woman. It is on this common basis of self-respect that an argument may be made that, on the whole, Africa today lives in real misery. The word misery, in Collin's English Thesaurus, has three sets of meanings:

1. Agony, anguish, depression, desolation, despair, discomfort, distress, gloom, grief, hardship, melancholy, sadness, sorrow, suffering, torment, torture, unhappiness, woe, wretchedness;

2. Affliction, bitter pill (Inf.), burden, calamity, catastrophe, curse, disaster, hardship, load, misfortune, ordeal, sorrow, trial, tribulation, trouble, woe;

3. Destitution, indigence, need, penury, poverty, privation, sordidness, squalor, want, wretchedness.....

The fact that one is an African must not be an excuse for not questioning issues that bring shame and misery to the continent. On the contrary, it should be our duty to be concerned with our dignity and the children we bring into this world as Africans. Our generation must not dodge the questions that earlier generations failed to address that affect Africa's present and future condition.

More than six million Africans are in destitute material situations – as IDPs (displaced from their homes and or villages) who live entirely dependent upon others' pity.[37] Africa has two and a half million refugees who are either on the continent or in distant lands where they must start new lives from scratch in unfamiliar environments. On average, there are over 50,000 patients for every doctor in Africa. According to the World Health Organization (WHO) 2007 child birth statistics, in Sierra Leone, 1 in 8 mothers died compared to 1 in 48,000 in Ireland! Out of every 1000 live births in Africa, 136 children die before reaching their fifth birthday. Out of every 100,000 women, 820 die during childbirth, while out of every 1000 mothers, only 103 are aged between 15 and 19. Access to secondary and tertiary education is only possible for 38% of males and 30% of female youths in Africa. The average rate of illiteracy is 32.8% and 50.1% among men and women, respectively. Scenes and printed media reports about places such as Darfur, Somalia, Eastern Congo (DRC), and Northern Uganda have continued to shock the world for the last seven years. Civil wars in Rwanda, Burundi, Liberia and Sierra Leone, to mention but a few, left hundreds of thousands dead, with those

37   https://www.statista.com/statistics/1232812/african-countries-hosting-most-refugees/

that survived living in abject poverty in addition to the rest of all human deprivation. Over 50% of Africans live on less than one dollar a day.

For most of the last half-century, to be anybody or to do anything in Africa, manhood has been the central criterion. While womanhood, on the other hand, has been a disqualification in almost every sphere of human endeavour. The misery in which the large majority of African people live today results from men's self-arrogated superior physical capability, courage, intelligence and willpower – which should be added to the marginalization and objectification of women. Aren't 'male dominance' and misery linked?

3. *The consequences of male military power and heroism in Africa*

Military coup d'états from the mid-60s to the present have embodied manhood in its true physical and masculine form in Africa. From Joseph Désiré Mobutu's coup d'état of 1965 followed by Major General J. A. Ankrah's in 1966 that ousted Kwame Nkrumah, generals like Idi Amin Dada, Siad Barre, Juvenal Habyarimana, Mengestu Haile Mariem, Fidel Bodel Bokassa, Eyadema Eyasingbe, Nimiery and others, joined by less graded soldiers such as Sergeant Samuel Kanyon Doe all took power. The culmination of this 'warrior leader' manhood driven rule on the continent occurred in 1975 when the Organization of African Unity (OAU) made General Idi Amin Dada its chairman for the year. Only one leader objected to this decision by the continent. The catastrophic results of this manhood put in charge of people's destinies continue in the countries concerned. Not surprisingly, many today question the wisdom of leaders staying in office for so long.

Nevertheless, some isolated exceptions to the general destructive nature of military leadership in Africa must be cited: Egypt's Gamal Abdel Nasser, Burkina Faso's Thomas Sankara who, like civilian Patrice Lumumba decades before him, did not live to see his projects his people come to pass; Nigeria's General Yakub Gowon, Ghana's Jerry Rawlings, Zimbabwe's Robert Mugabe, Uganda's Yoweri Museveni and Libya's Muammar al-Gaddafi. What is outstanding in the acts and omissions of these leaders is the shared negligible readiness to involve women in critical decision-making processes. A woman was occasionally appointed to some public office as a minister, vice president, but without genuinely delegating powers to them.

The perception that African men are invincible beings, particularly in leading nations out of bondage, poverty, insecurity, and other aspects of dehumanization, proved to be questionable after the effects of several military juntas in control. Academicians were almost always sceptical and often challenged soldiers in this regard. One distinguished African thinker, Wole Soyinka, published a novel, *The Lion and the Jewel* as early as 1963. Even though it was not an obvious political piece of writing, Wole Soyinka's initiative had merit in that he wanted the competition or demonstration of superior abilities by individuals to be shifted from the purely physical plane to the intellectual. In his novel, Wole Soyinka contrasted the young with the elderly using male and female characters. In this regard, Wole Soyinka was dealing with gender issues! He had the two male characters as real human beings in their competition over a beautiful young woman. However, he did not give the female character the attributes of a human person but instead, the reader is presented with a 'pearl' – in other words – an inert natural element or object. Wole Soyinka depicts the female character as something one can acquire – a 'jewel' – leaving the aspects of real brain work and rivalry between the two men – the elderly man as the Lion while the young man is left in his human form. Wole Soyinka's story beautifully conveys the message that even relatively feeble bodied persons may perform far more effectively in critical situations to achieve the desired objectives than the apparently physically sound and sophisticated. The elderly and simple villager outwits the confident and assuming young educated man who is freshly returned from abroad.

From the gender perspective, however, as with many men, Wole Soyinka fell right into the 'womanhood trap' with his comic story! His initiative was heroic in that it sought to show that Africa must take the competition from the physical or muscle dimensions to the mental. What it fatally suffered from was his not being able to go beyond men's power monopoly. To Wole Soyinka, womanhood was synonymous with weakness and gullibility. The reader is left with an objectified woman – a jewel – tricked, used (actually raped), and placed where an enterprising man chooses. In this particular case, she is taken into a polygamous marital cul-de-sac to become the Lion's possession, a prey. There is no hint of the gross human rights violation committed by the hero against the hardly adult female person. Above all, the brilliance of 'the Lion' is, in fact, celebrated in Wole Soyinka's story. Indeed, the conclusion of this story shows that Wole Soyinka's initiative only served to reinforce the presumptuous male view that women are no match for men's abilities – and in this particular scenario, especially intellectually! Wole Soyinka missed an opportunity to demonstrate that women too can have remarkable mental power or resourcefulness. A person of exceptional talent and literary enlightenment, Wole Soyinka must have known that three and a half centuries earlier, William Shakespeare, between 1596 and 1604, like him had entertained the English theatre-goers using both men and women, young and old as well as both white and black characters. The intellectual power of youthful Portia in 'The Merchant of Venice' displayed in the trial scene astounded elderly Shylock, a man himself and all the onlookers. Again, the unprecedented ethical and racially unprejudiced views exhibited by the youthful Desdemona to her own father and everyone around – including her husband, the celebrated military General Othello in the play 'Othello' are inescapably outstanding. Closer to home, this time in Africa itself, Okot p'Bitek, in his poem 'Song of Lawino' (1967), was to abundantly demonstrate that womanhood also carries remarkable cultural, political and socio-economic intellectual abilities which are often claimed to be exclusive properties of manhood. Specifically, Lawino challenges leadership by sophisticated men on the shameful social condition Africans were caught up in. It was Lawino, Okot p'Bitek's village woman who articulated these words:

"Why do they split up the army
Into two hostile groups?

...while the pythons of sickness
Swallow the children
    And the buffaloes of poverty
Knock the people down
And ignorance stands there
Like an elephant"?[38].

The message about how women's talent and ability can come into prominence was brought out even more powerfully in a widely recognized piece of theatrical art by Robert Wise produced in 1965 as the 'Sound of Music' film, which many have either watched or heard about. In that story, Maria, also an ordinary village young woman hired as a nanny in a home where a bunch of seven impossible children and their arrogant military father who receives her with ridicule, amazes everyone in the end. Because of her unbending character, Maria had been thrown out of a woman's place, the convent. Maria would not take orders from her military employer either. She transformed the entire world around the widower and his children. This was womanhood coming out as care, firmness, intelligence and perseverance – not physical force.

This is not to say that the abilities women may possess cannot be possessed by men as well. One critical domain in human existence where women have demonstrated indisputable superiority in playing a role is 'bearing and rearing children' or, perhaps, laying the foundation for humanity's future. Yet, women have attained excellence in this field of caring for humanity at their tender age only through cultural or

38 Quoted from G-C Mutiso in "Social Political Thought in African Literature: Weusi?" – Chapter 6 – The Role of Women, pp56. Footnote 17 and 19 refer to Okot p'Bitek, Song of Lawino (Nairobi: East African Publishing House, 1967 p.181

social preparation. There is no biological ground that predisposes women to play this role or, conversely, which makes men incapable of playing it – at least not in the present technological age. That men could do just as well in this, if they really want to, was once again powerfully demonstrated by another playwright, Robin Williams, in his 1993 film entitled 'Mrs Doubtfire'. Again, many will be familiar with the amusing hairy-legged old nurse whom the children absolutely adored.

These two important works of art, produced by men of talent in the entertainment industry should help us see the hollowness of certain assertions about so-called women's and men's natural roles. The old saying still stands that 'What a man can do, a man can do' except that the language was not yet gendered. Similarly, questions must be raised about sexism in traditional religious jargon. Are women not made subordinate to men in prayer when we use expressions such as *'Our Heavenly father'* and 'Our Father who art in heaven'?

4. Male power monopoly and consequences on Africa's populations

There is little evidence to show that manhood on its own, even when combined with the advantage of intellectual preparation, brings about the remedy to Africa's miserable conditions of existence. Three experiences of long and uninterrupted male civilian leadership in Africa – namely Liberia, Cameroon, and Rwanda- are examined below to show the results of this.

Below are two graphs showing Africa's position against other regions of the world on two governance subjects:

Figure 2: Budget expenditure on social protection as per cent of GDP by regions of the world, 2004-2007

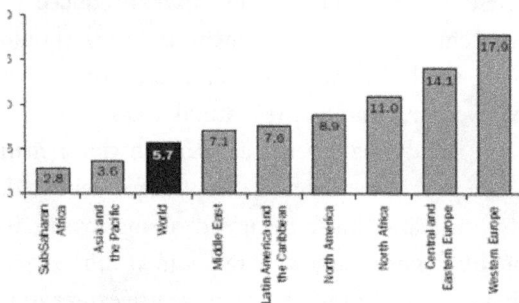

t 6.1   Budget expenditure on social protection as per cent of GDP by regions of the world, 2004-2007

: Based on data from ILO (2010)

Figure 3: Gross enrolment ratios for pre-primary education by regions of the world

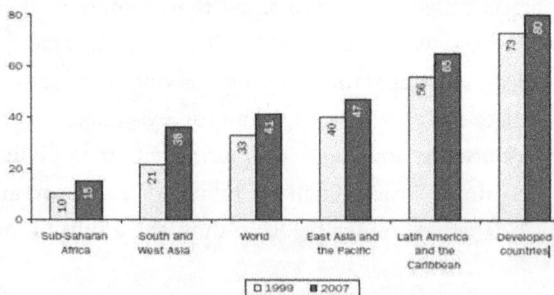

Chart 4.3   Gross enrolment ratios for pre-primary education by regions of the world

Source: Based on data from UNESCO (2010)

A hundred and thirty-three years of civilian male rule in one African country

In 1847 Liberia declared its independence from the American Colonizing Society. The settler descendants of ex-slaves from the United States of America assumed control of the country from that date until the 1980 coup d'état. For all that period of time, male civilian political power had been practically held only by the settler community. Some notable Liberian writers have said that the 1980 uprising – also referred to as the 'rice riots' which marked the end of the quasi-exclusively Americo-Liberian True Whig Party's power monopoly was a reaction to the impoverishment and denigration of the indigenous population – that constituted approximately 95% of Liberians. Available literature suggests that for most Liberians, the 150 years of civilian 'manhood' driven national leadership led to the misery they live in today. Tragically, Samuel Doe and Charles Taylor only exacerbated the conditions of existence for Liberians. The nation's agony culminated in a high price of 200,000 lives perishing before the war could be stopped in August 2003. The loss of such a huge number of citizens by a country remains a 'never again' political reference – not only for Liberians but for all of Africa and the rest of the world. Three points need to be noted for the case of Liberia: First, that men or 'manhood' monopolized decision making and controlled political power in a nation for over a century but essentially prepared the people for hardship and self-destruction, although not knowingly. Secondly, physical might, whether exercised by a half illiterate or highly educated person, was not in itself the solution to Liberian's most crucial need – life, health and self-realization plus security. Thirdly and finally, the case of Liberia shows that providing protection – i.e. safety and security to a county's population goes far beyond what the armed defence forces of the country can do. Two years after the war ended, Liberia's elections in October of 2005 produced Africa's first test case of womanhood in control. A woman, Maama Ellen Johnson Sirleaf, assumed the office of President and Head of State for the first time in Liberia's and Africa's history. Lawino and her creator Okot p'Tek as well as Tereza Nanziri from Uganda must have rolled over in their graves at this announcement.

In January 2006, Africa's first woman president was sworn in. President Ellen Johnson Sirleaf's Liberia was now clearly a post-war nation. What is more, militarily, approximately 15,000 blue helmets together with hundreds of highly professional police officers from some of the best national police services in the world were also deployed in Liberia. This was for security purposes and for the protection of citizens' lives as well as their property. For a country with a population of just over three million, this military presence was enormous. Closer analysis of the effectiveness of conventional defence arrangements such as these by nations to provide security and safety of citizens' lives reveals that they can be utterly impotent in some critical respects. The realities on the ground show that gender and social protection issues, in general, must not be minimized by an over-concentration on the military or physical aspects of citizens' protection.

Between 2005 and 2008 alone, an average of 21,686 lives in Liberia were lost per year because of the very high maternal mortality ratio and infant mortality rate. Although losing 200,000 human lives during the 14 years of war shocked Liberians and the world, if the above-estimated death figures a year are multiplied by the seven years (2003 - 2010), the total comes to 151,802. Compared to the figures of 14 years of war, the figures depicting death during the time of peace are a third higher, i.e. 303,604! What is the explanation for this? The maternal death ratio and the under-five infant mortality rate were 990/100,000 and 145/1000, respectively. Since the number of live births for the period 2005-2008 was 140,000, the country lost 1,386 mothers and 20,300 under-five children in that period. Other factors connected with citizens' low level of access, especially mothers and children to basic social services, i.e. doctors, midwives, nurses, and adequate feeding, aggravate the conditions of survival for the poor who make up the large majority of rural citizens in Liberia. The doctor/patients ratio is 1:33, with 300 in Liberia, against the 1:390 in the United States. It is only 1:170 in Cuba. Africa's misery acuteness in this regard was captured in 2007 by WHO's Director, Department of Making Pregnancy Safer, Dr Monir Islam:

> "A woman's risk of dying in pregnancy or childbirth varied between countries: it was greatest in Africa and Asia. In Africa, 1 in 26 women died as a result of pregnancy; in Asia 1 in 120. In Sierra Leone 1 in 8 mothers died compared to 1 in 48,000 in Ireland. But even within countries, there were large differences between rich and

poor people, and between the urban and
rural population".

The Liberian case helps to reveal how reality very often
eludes peoples' critical notice. It is rare that deaths that
are not related to war or other massive catastrophes
such as the tsunami in Japan are discussed in the media.

An African Country's Forty Years
of Peaceful Sovereign Existence

Since the time of its independence from France in
1960, Cameroon has had only two civilian male
political leaders. It has naturally always had a Ministry
of Defence with a fully equipped army. Except for
the brief military showing of teeth to its neighbour
Nigeria, over the Bakassi peninsular dispute that dated
from 1913 that was finally peacefully adjudicated
by the International Court of Justice in 2002, the
Cameroonian army has primarily been a symbolic and
ceremonial entity. Despite this, however, each year's
funds are allocated for its maintenance. For the year
2007, for instance, Cameroon's military budget was
over half a billion (US$556,270,000), constituting
1.3% of the national budget. Many African nations
maintain similar armies 'for the nation's security, safety
and protection'. However, what the statistics say
about the actual safety and survival of the population
in Cameroon that year is quite a different story. In

2007 alone, 4,212 adult women Cameroonians died. Additionally, 19,700 young children lost their lives. The latter group was of citizens under five years of age, i.e. all non-combatants. In this case, too, like the situation in post-war Liberian, the deaths were not the kind that even the best-armed men could prevent! Maternal mortality and child mortality in the country were the two causes.

Many other African countries like Cameroon and Liberia continuously suffer these huge losses in women and children year after year. These facts are documented in the World Health Organization's (WHO) and the United Nations Development Program's (UNDP) Human Development Index Reports under maternal mortality ratio and infant mortality rates. In the case of Cameroon, the report covering the 1990-2008 period shows the maternity mortality ratio to have been 600 per 100,000 live births (higher than the world average of 400 deaths). The same source gives the under-five children mortality rate for 2005 and 2008, averaging about 65.84 per 1000 live births. The average figure of live births per year was 687,000 over that period. It follows that Cameroon lost 45,232 children under five years of age in 2007. Based on the above figures, for the period 2003-2008, 320,000 children died in Cameroon, with at least 40,000 dying annually. If the total of 4,212 women who died per year due to pregnancy-related causes over that period is added to this figure, the total number of citizens who died in Cameroon over the eight years is (320,000 +(4,212x8)) = 357,712.

By any standard, this is a very heavy loss of lives for a country, yet these figures are not inclusive of other

deaths resulting from accidents, suicide, malaria, HIV/
AIDS, and other crimes. The final figure could be well
over half a million deaths – in Cameroon's 'peaceful'
existence.

Rwanda – fast rising from the ashes? A unique case in Africa's suffering experience.

Of all independent African countries, Rwanda has the
most recent and highest human death rate per time
unit which was experienced during the 1994 genocide.
The death toll was estimated at a million lives, all
within a hundred days. Calculations suggest that the
killings occurred at the startling rate of a death every
10 seconds. There are several striking aspects of post-
genocide leadership in Rwanda. Whatever the reasons
behind his policies, President Paul Kagame comes out
as an innovative male African politician whose thoughts
are likened to those of late Thomas Sankara and the
architect of modern-day Singapore, H.E. Lee Kuan
Yew. President Kagame's penchant for involving women
in state business came out during the 2008 general
elections, Rwanda with 56% of the seats in parliament,
became the country with the highest number of female
representation in the legislature worldwide. This
followed earlier radical changes in the laws, which,
prior to the genocide, disallowed the inheritance of
property by widows or girl orphans. Education is the
other domain where the Rwandan leadership sets
unprecedented standards in its determination to bring
about gender equality and equity in children's access to
schooling. There appear to be some similarities in the

approach adopted by both Rwanda and Liberia, two countries that were seriously afflicted by civil wars. It is as though the huge loss of human lives makes the leadership more appreciative of the fact that people are the nation's most valuable resource. This, in turn, would lead to people-centred policies, particularly for women and children. It is an established fact that a well-nourished mother guarantees the baby's good feeding since the latter relies on the mother's breast. The nexus between the pro-women government actions and child rights or wellbeing come out very clearly in the data on Rwanda and Liberia, according to African Child Protection Forum Report 2011.

Figure 4: A graph showing the leading positions that the two war-affected countries Liberia and Rwanda, occupy on early child'en's primary education.

Chart 5.5   Total aid for basic education per primary school-age child in countries with GDP per capita of less than USD 500, 2007

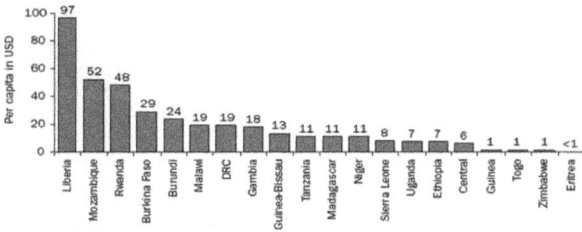

Source: Based on data from UNESCO (2010)

Figure 5: A graph showing the leading positions Liberia and Rwanda occupy on the continent in health budgeting

Table 3.2 Government net per capita expenditure on health in comparison with per capita expenditure from all sources, for countries that have met the Abuja target, 2008

Country	Health expenditure as % of total government expenditure (Per cent)	Per capita expenditure on health from all sources (In USD)	Government's net per capita expenditure on health (In USD)
Rwanda	18.9	48	23
Liberia	16.8	26	9
Tanzania	16.2	25	16
Zambia	15.2	68	42

Source: Based on data from WHO (2010)

Matrix borrowed from African Children Protection Forum Report 2011 – pp62.

Despite being one of the countries with the lowest GDP on the continent, Rwanda allocated 18.9% of the national budget to health, surpassing the Abuja Commitment of 15%, which only four countries achieved in 2008. That Liberia follows after with the next highest budget allocation towards health in Africa deserves commendation, considering the nation's limited resources after the recent war. It is the combination of a deliberate desire to involve more women in decision-making processes, prioritizing citizen's health needs and facilitating children's education, particularly the girl child, which becomes the focus of the rest of this paper.

5. Would a positive view of womanhood by men help reduce people's misery in Africa?

Courage, brain power and capability to withstand excruciating pain have come to be regarded as a natural tendency for men until now – as demonstrated during circumcision rites without the use of pain killers. However, what has not been done is to find out whether no evidence exists to prove that women too are endowed with the same qualities – maybe to an even higher degree. On courage, France's Jeanne d'Arc as a military commander during the 15th century is well known to most readers. Records indicate that famous male political leaders such as Emperor Napoleon Bonaparte emulated Jeanne d'Arc. If it is African examples of Jeanne d'Arc who must be mentioned, Professor Ali Mazrui did so ten years ago in July 1991 when he referred to Uganda's Alice Lakwena as the Jeanne of Arc of Acholi land after naming Alice Lanshina in Zambia, whose willpower as a religious non-conformist led her then country's president, Kenneth Kaunda to order his troops to shoot her and her followers. Ms Tereza Nanziri stood Amin's fury to the point of dying for her determination to defend a student at Makerere University in Uganda.

As for bearing bodily pain, is there any doubt about the extreme and paralyzing pain a woman endures during childbirth? Did traditional African mothers know of painkillers? Moreover, unlike men, women go through this agony repeatedly – often more than six times, depending on how many children they bear. To compare the one-time pain experienced by a man during circumcision with what women endure almost throughout their lifetime is like making a bad joke. There are cases where labour pains torture a mother for an entire day or even longer. This superiority complex based on muscle power has been rendered considerably irrelevant by technology when comparing men and women at any rate. What is required of men and women alike is mainly brainpower, sharp eyes, ears and fingers.

With the definition of misery stated earlier in this chapter, we see that to fight it in Africa, all the continent's human talent should be mobilized and fully utilised. However, this has not been done since women were largely considered unequal to men and found to be less useful. Therefore, they were treated as immature at best or bluntly as children, i.e. they were viewed as unable to contribute to society's construction.

Recognizing womanhood with its particular values and unique capabilities will release a huge new current of energy from women that will become available to complement, if not boost, men's efforts. Womanhood – until now a contemptuous label of disqualification – will become a critical factor in reducing society's misery. How will this happen? We now turn to this question.

Recognition of women's exceptional talents and value in certain domains of human life: For example, the bearing and rearing of the future Africans we need. African men must have the courage to openly acknowledge that women are demonstrably more gifted than men in certain areas of human endeavour. One of these is the science of bearing and rearing the human race, which is, in fact, the preparation of the most vital national resources in any country. The immediate results from such a change in men's attitude will be multi-dimensional and beneficial to the entire continent.

Fathers should start viewing every single girl child as the 'goose that lays the golden egg' and stop regarding them as dispensable members of society. This will lead parents towards prioritizing girls' wellbeing and education, which in some instances might even mean recognizing the need to ensure additional care for the girl child. Today, much of the misery described above results from the fact that a very large majority of mothers are illiterate and thus unaware of many simple things, new ideas, are in poor health and know very little about their bodies. In this condition, they cannot fully help society and are instead part of the problem. Where and when men need to be helped or are misguided, the offer of assistance to them is limited. Women's attitude towards abuse (being battered by their husbands) for different reasons in several African countries illustrate this helplessness. The relevance of education as a foundation for able and quality women in a country becomes more apparent.

Denying a daughter education exposes her to all forms of misery and abuse in life. According to the table below (UNICEF's 2008 statistics), the illiteracy rate for girls in Mali is 80.6%, while in Rwanda, it is at 33.9%.

Table 2: Comparing educational opportunities to children, illiteracy status and the national gross income per capita in four countries

Country	Year	Illiteracy rate %		Mean years of schooling	Gross national income/capita ($)
		Male	Female		
Mali	2008	M60.5	**F80.6**	1.4	1,171
Benin	2008	M46.5	**F71.9**	3.5	1,499
Rwanda	2008	M25.2	**F33.9**	3.3	1,190
Tanzania	2008	M21.0	**F33.7**	5.1	1,344

The consequences of the deficient levels in girls' schooling and their illiteracy rate are clear.

Women in Africa deserve to be viewed as mothers, wives, sisters, aunts or daughters. Being the principal decision-makers so far, men have been responsible for a lot of what is wrong. We do not criminalise anyone since it was not done in bad faith. Nevertheless, what must be said is that what has happened in many countries – denying girls education is exactly what the apartheid regime in South Africa did during the '70s – leading to the well-known student uprisings. At one point, under the Bantustan system, the state budgetary allocation per child for the school year 1978-79 was R724 for each white pupil, while only R71.28 was allocated for each black pupil. In effect, this meant spending only $1 on the education of a black child while $10 were spent on each white child. The long term consequences of these discriminative policies on black South Africans were clear when in 1994, the country became independent. Special measures to catch up on and empower black South Africans were prioritised. The effects of poverty, disease and ignorance on mothers in Africa must be fought through an education strategy. This view was captured by one of Africa's new generation of brilliant leaders in the mid-80s, namely, Yoweri Museveni, who in 1992 recognized education's vital relevance in the emancipation of people when he said:

> 'Our biggest problem in the third world today is not one of lack of resources, it is lack of technology. The fact is that we do not have the technical know-how is itself caused by a lack of education. Our people are not educated and they are, therefore, not able to utilize their brains to transform their lives. This is the biggest crisis we are facing today.'[39]

39 Yoweri K. Museveni, What is AFRICA'S PROBLEM – NRA Publications: Confront Real Issues, pp180.

Our own position is that educating a nation's children is the pivot of development in all aspects of the word. However, because of the failure to pay enough attention to the special challenges girls face in accessing education, special gender mainstreaming must be integrated in any national education policy for the right results. This aspect is still weak in Africa. Yoweri Museveni's wisdom was complemented and buttressed by the admonition below from one of Africa's most influential respected thinkers and educators today:

> 'Gender planning is perhaps the most serious of all the omissions in Africa's political and economic reforms....We need to add gender planning if Africa's grand design for the 1990s and the 21st Century is to become comprehensive enough and fundamental enough to tilt the balance in favour of genuine transformation.'[40]

6. Effectively defending and protecting people's lives in African countries: Undoing the misery trap.

Women's high capabilities in dealing with some of the challenges often faced by humanity have been hinted at above. The constantly very high number of deaths amongst women and children in Africa is undoubtedly one of these challenges. This is a problem that is inextricably linked to the very high fertility rate and the poverty in which most African women live, compared to the other regions of the world.

---

40 Professor Ali Mazrui in 'CONCLUSION' to the 1991 Guardian Lecture referred to under The Black Women and the Problem of Gender ... delivered on July 4, 1991

The critical issue for African men and women to realize and focus on is the central role a woman plays in any strategy designed to extricate Africa from the misery and death of children and mothers. Until now, women have been largely disempowered and made to be part of the problem instead of being seen as part of the solution. We now present what is the way out of the womanhood trap:

Once conception of a child occurs, there is a 50% possibility that the child will be a girl. To ensure that the baby will not have avoidable deficiencies, every protective measure by both parents must be taken. Appropriate nutritional, ante-natal medical visits and the best physical and psychological environment are to be provided. Should the parents require state assistance or loans from employers, this should be provided as a national priority. All this will significantly count towards the overall fitness and wellbeing of the child, something that is doubly important in the case of the baby turning out to be a girl, i.e. a future key player in society in many ways.

In the interest of the child, parents, especially the mother, must be spared stressful physical and mental states, which ultimately manifest themselves in children's low IQ, among other things, the best medical attention, sufficient nourishment and conducive home, as well as family conditions, should deliberately be provided by the parents – if possible with state supportive legal and financial arrangements. The above conditions presuppose that in all African countries, every child is invariably registered at birth. Furthermore, all children have safe and appropriate pre-school caring at the end of which they must all go to school. Investing in countries' human resources is extremely necessary and must start from the cradle.

Figure 6: Graph illustrating benefits from early care for a child.

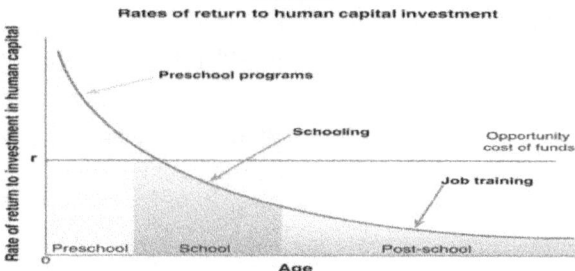

Rates of return to human capital investment

(Source Heckman and Mastrov - 2007 also used in the ACPF Report 2011)

The critical importance of adequately investing in citizens' infancy and early childhood to build a healthy, strong and intelligent competent nation is well illustrated in the diagram above. Poor health, together with malnutrition in Africa, does not only cause deaths among children. Those who survive show a lower than required level of mental ability to perform in school. For girls, failure at school robs the nation of quality mothers who in turn give insufficient support to their own children. Sadly, this is commonly the present condition.

If parents adopt just the above measures in Africa, the present alarming high fertility rate will significantly drop. Africa's girl children will be busy attending school and acquiring knowledge as well as skills to live decent lives instead of being dragged into often forced premature marriages. Unwanted pregnancies, maternal deaths and related infant mortality will diminish. The ability to read and acquire basic knowledge in biology and arithmetic will free girls from the high incidence of dropping out of school, arising from avoidable pregnancies. Enrolment in secondary schools and girls' performance and completion rates in secondary and tertiary learning institutions will rise throughout the continent.

Africa must deliberately raise the general quality level of mothers. Unenlightened mothers undermine Africa's success in areas where other societies do miraculously well. An educated and enlightened woman makes a mother an asset, first to herself and then to her husband as an equal partner. She is an invaluable asset to the children and to the country; an educated woman is the kingpin in the development chassis. This is why investing in children as soon as they are conceived – not only after they are born – must be a priority.

Each one of us speaks a 'mother tongue'! Do we ever stop to think about why it is not a father tongue? This is a stamp of womanhood that each walking human being carries – proudly too. Communication – 'speech' which is the critical faculty possessed by human beings and distinguishes us from other animals – is primarily passed on from one human being to the other by the woman. Able and outstanding citizens mirror the qualities or deficiencies of their parents, but mostly those of mothers. It is interesting to note that the Baganda, Basamia, the Spanish and the French share the same expression; '*Nnyoko*'; '*Maao*'; '*Tu Madre*' and '*Ta mère*' respectively, to insult another! This is an undeniable assertion that we are what our mothers make us – either better or worse human beings.

The story of little Moses in the Old Testament is one such example. The preservation of his life and his rearing hinged on a woman – a daughter of the Pharaoh who at the time took an interest in protecting the abandoned boy child. Emperor Napoleon Bonaparte's early life story tells of his father's early death, leaving him under the firm personality of the mother. The story of the Great Chief Shaka Zulu childhood and upbringing is similar; raised by a largely unaided mother. These examples of women's contribution to greatness in history may seem remote. In our own time, the story of a Liberian girl child – Angie Elizabeth Brooks, born in 1928, powerfully shows the unique value of having an intelligent and able mother. The list of these examples is endless. I would be irredeemably failing if I concluded my list of examples without citing one of today's greatest world leaders, the former president of the United States of America, Mr Barack Hussein Obama!

I urge all men to take heed of these lessons. Until now, our fault in Africa has been to reject women as able partners in anything, and we have paid the price – a very high one. We got caught in the trap of our own making. My experience in human rights work showed that quite a number of women are caught in the same trap. The struggle to empower women calls for a joint men/women effort.

Women are the pivot of our emancipation and development, starting from families to key state institutions. For this to be realized, girls must be treated not only the way their brothers are but in some situations allow preferential concessions to be made as a deliberate measure to fast-track their progress, in view of the neglect they have been subjected to in the past. We should look at Rwanda as a 'best practices case'. While boosting the educational facilities and opportunities for girls who require time, Rwandans have fielded able women as candidates in the countryside, and by 2020, over 60% of the members in their legislature were women. Let women express their views on burning national issues as well. There are issues where certain aspects of the problem are not obvious to male decision-makers, even when the intellectual capacities are clearly high. The law on inheritance in Rwanda is one such example.

When women acquire the same level of education, professional experience, the exercise of power control, decision-making responsibilities as men, as well as economic performance in terms of GDP, will definitely shoot up all around Africa. The levels of ill-health will fall with the availability of medical personnel, and the economic means to pay them decent salaries will rise. This is the opposite of misery as the conditions of living will inevitably improve for everyone. Although Africa is rich and has the potential to make its people happy, Africans are not at peace, dignified or materially comfortable. The problem so far has been leaders – with almost men everywhere not making appropriate choices at the right time and in the proper places. Rwanda, Botswana, Tanzania and Liberia are showing signs of a radical change in budgeting priorities.

Table 3: Comparing statistics of six selected African countries, showing their resources and social challenge levels.

Country	Population (million)[41]	GD[42] US$	MM R	IMR (<5's)	Patient-Dr Ratio[43]	IoD[44]	M/F illiteracy (%)[45]		Def-Budget (NB%)
Cameroon	18,17	2,219	600	131	50,300	54.7	16.8	29.2	1.5
Mali	11,96	1,207	830	194	12,500	51.44	60.5	80.6	1.9
Tanzania	39,45	1,426	790	104	50,000	56.3	20	41.1	1.1
Burundi	8,17	403	970	168	33,500	62.7	40	51.8	4.0
Liberia	3,57	400	990	145	33,500	57.7	24.8	57.3	0.6
Rwanda	9,46	1,102	540	112	20,000	54.4	22.1	32.3	1.5

From the statistical table above, it is clear that the problem is not a lack of resources. The countries which have done best at providing social protection for their people and whose school enrolment figures are highest are not those with the highest GDP. Cameroon, with a GDP of $2,219 – i.e. more than twice that of Rwanda ($1,102) has a higher maternal mortality ratio, infant mortality rate and a poorer doctor/patients ratio! Similarly, Liberia, which has only a third of Mali's GDP ($400 against $1,207), has a lower infant mortality rate and a literacy rate that is almost three times higher. The worst affected in both examples are the women and children. Men bear the greatest responsibility to bring about the necessary change.

In conclusion, this chapter pleads that men's view of womanhood is scientifically wrong, is without justification, and is detrimental to Africa's human development. Given an equally enabling environment, particularly in this technological age, men and women can do the same things, and in some instances, women with the same training, encouragement, and opportunities may accomplish tasks better in society's interest. Finally, all Africans (both men and women) should adopt an approach that sees the opposite sex as an indispensable complement to building national well-being, wealth, peace, and security. Until now, largely inadvertently, men have blocked this complementarity by excluding women from the running of affairs, leading to self-inflicted misery for decades but together, we shall stand stronger and happier.

VII

THE ABUSE OF AFRICAN MIGRANT WOMEN WORKERS AND THE EFFORTS OF THE UNITED NATIONS

The wisdom of ancient Africans is rarely evoked by experts in discussions concerning human rights issues that involve the affliction of societies, or big proportions of populations in Africa. To some, this is normal because there was never 'science', or 'thought' in Africa, in the way it developed within societies in Europe or elsewhere. For others, this is due to ignorance of the existence of any such "wisdom" that could be cited in serious scientific debate.

This chapter proposes that the abuse of African migrant women workers is in fact, unlike what many may think, contrary to precolonial African moral teachings based on 'Ubuntu'. In the search for solutions to the plight of African migrant women workers, the chapter sheds light on Africa's positive traditional values as seen through the works of ethical thinkers like the late Chinua Achebe. The chapter discusses the similarities between Africa's traditions and the United Nations' efforts to mitigate the abuse migrant African women are subjected to.

If **abuse** in this context means failure or refusal by State institutions or their agents to adhere to or respect human rights norms and standards vis-à-vis women workers in Africa, what does this mean exactly for African people today?

Criticisms about gross denial of human rights to women and in particular migrant women workers has tended to be based solely on prescriptions in the Universal Declaration of Human Rights and other subsequent treaties or conventions brought into being through the United Nations system emanating from it. Yet, in spite of those conventions – many of them subscribed to and were ratified by Governments – abuse and denial of human rights continue unabated in Africa.

Worse still, there are some "Afrocentric" thinkers who have even argued that the said "rights" notions advanced through the United Nations are alien to Africa, and must not therefore be imposed on peoples who only recently freed themselves from Western colonial impositions. Africa has her own cultural norms and values to guide a harmonious and safe collective existence for its people.

The issue of migrant women workers' abuse in Africa today must be seriously addressed. If truly understood as it is, it negates decency, it is unethical, inhuman. It could even be said to be contrary to African fundamental moral teaching, based on Ubuntu that sustained societal cohesion prior to Western cultural, religious, and administrative as well as the monetization influences. Africans had respectable, old civilizations before the European civilizing projects!

In this discussion, it is argued therefore, that allowing the abuses of migrant women workers in our midst to go unsanctioned, firstly contravenes ancient African human rights cannons, and only violates modern human rights norms in the second place. This must be understood before the discussion can proceed. For a semblance of the centrality of African positive traditional values, this discussion recognises Nigeria's venerated departed ethical thinker, novelist and our teacher, Chinua Achebe.

Born in Africa in 1930 and departed to re-join our ancestors in March 2013, Chinua Achebe left his ringing voice in **Things Fall Apart** and **No longer at Ease**. He, unlike many of the educated among us, recognised the importance of African traditional cultural values which should guide our lifestyles, and urged us not to rush into mimicking what is modern. This is not to say that Chinua Achebe was blind to what wasn't right within some of our African traditional practices, nor that in his endeavour to give a central place to original African wisdom, he was alone. This same call was made by Ngugi Wa Thiong'o in Kenya, Cheikh Anta Diop in Senegal, Wangari Muta Maathai in Kenya, Amadou Hampâté Bâ in Mali, and Ki-Zerbo Joseph in Burkina Faso, to name but a few. For the specific purpose of this discussion, let us travel together about eight hundred years back in our African history to the time of Emperor Sundiata Keita, around the year 1200AD. This time in African human experience will contextualize this discussion on the abuse of migrant women workers in Africa.

How did ancient Africans view cruelty, injustice, and indecent treatment of (alien) women prior to the 'introduction' of European notions of human rights to the African continent? To answer this question we need to refer to the existence of the Kurukan Fuga Charter.[41] This is an ancient human rights declaration dating back to the same period when people in England presented the Magna Carter to their King. The Charter of Kurukan Fuga was made by Sundiata Keita in the year 1235 and had 44 articles, three of which are of special relevance to this discussion. The treatment of women, slaves, and foreigners is covered in that charter by articles 14, 20 and 24 respectively as follows:

(1) "Never <u>offend</u> women, our mothers."
    (*N'offensez jamais les femmes, nos mères.*)
(2) "Do not <u>ill-treat</u> the slaves...." (*Ne maltraitez, pas les esclaves....*)
(3) "In Mandé never <u>do wrong</u> to foreigners..."
    (*Ne faites jamais du tort aux étrangers*)

Due to these citations having gone through translation at least three times to bring us a message originally orally transmitted across eight centuries, I decided to focus my attention on the verb which is recurrently prohibited in the three articles – i.e. "offend", and sought to see its exact current meaning in English. In the Longman Dictionary of the English Language[42] it is explained as follows:

---

41 The Charter of Kurukan Fuga, is a version collected in Guinea at the end of a concerting regional workshop between traditional and modern communicators (Kankan: 3 - 12 March 1998). The traditionists are those who declined the texts; then it has been transcribed and translated, with the help of guinea linguists and under the supervision of Mr .Siriman Kouyaté-Magistrate and traditionalist (his family is guardian of the sosoba, in Niagasole, Guinea). Afterwards S. Kouyaté structured the charter, without falsifying the essential point; talking here about the modern judicial texts with a view to make readable for contemporization (the original text in Malinke is available on the digital data bank ARTO).

42 Longman Dictionary of the English Language (Major New Edition, 1994), pp1111

A: **1a** to break a moral or divine law; sin. **1b** to violate a law or rule; do wrong. **2a** to cause difficulty or discomfort; **2b** to cause displeasure or anger or vexation.

B: **1-** to cause pain or displeasure to; hurt **2-** to cause to feel indignation or disgust – usually by violation of what is descent or courteous.

On the basis of the above meaning, we deduce that ancient Africans forbade perpetrating violence against foreign (migrant) women slaves (workers) as it meant breaking moral or divine laws applicable to them, violating those laws or rules; causing difficulty and discomfort to them, hurting them, causing them to feel pain, displeasure and disgust.

Such an understanding of twelfth century African historical records on human rights norms, decisively shifts the argument by which modern Africans would seek to despise our traditions or accept not being referred to by Westerners, in recent declarations or conventions. Indeed it is here that the universality of the UDHR should become legitimate, as it reflects what Africans in fact already knew as humanity's requirements, and did hold them dear.

It is against the above illustration of Africa's old principles based on humanness or humanity – i.e. "ubuntu/obuntu", that we now turn to establishing what constitutes abuse or objectification of African migrant women workers today. To do so, a brief presentation of the factors which cause women to leave their home countries and migrate to distant and unknown lands, will help.

Although most available information on migration by researchers is seldom broken down to separately show male and female figures, the general agreement is that many women, just like men, leave home as a solution to difficulties experienced on the ground (within the family, uneasy marital situations, national economic hardship, or life-threatening conditions) in order to find a solution to them abroad. According to the International Labour Organisation (ILO) 2010 figures, there were a total of 5,236,000 domestic workers in Africa. Of these, 3,835,000, i.e. 73.2% were women. Further, while in Africa women domestic workers constituted 13.6% of female employed employees, men domestic workers accounted for only 1.8%.[43]

---

43 It should be noted here that the ILO statistics do not distinguish between domestic workers between migrant or local.

Figure 7: Distribution of domestic workors by sex and region, 2010

Figure 3.1   Distribution of domestic workers by sex and region, 2010

Distribution of domestic workers
by sex, 2010 estimates

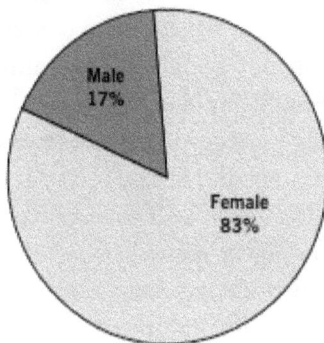

*Source: Domestic workers across the world: Global and regional
statistics and the extent of global protection, Figure 3.1, Chapter 3, pp21*

Migrant women working in foreign lands fall into
various categories on closer scrutiny. Some are
young, unmarried and without children while others
may be mature – often married and parents (with
or without children with them). These immigrant
women workers may also be further divided into
professional, highly qualified persons while others may
be unskilled labourers. Additionally, the classification
of immigrant women workers may be made in two
broader kinds - the 'legal' and 'illegal' immigrants. This
last categorization further enables us to gain a better
understanding of the category of the women that are

the most vulnerable among African women workers. In view of the breadth of this subject, we shall focus our attention on the abuses suffered by women migrant domestic workers. This isn't to suggest that the cruelty and dehumanisation of the migrant women workers employed in the entertainment, manufacturing, agricultural, seafaring and other industries aren't of equal concern. Similarly, the choice to concentrate on this category of migrant women workers must not be taken to mean that highly qualified professional and skilled women who go abroad for work experience no gender based or xenophobic abuses.

Another point which deserves to be made here is that United Nations Agencies specialists on the rights of migrant workers, provide information indicating that African migrant (domestic) workers are subjected to cruel conditions of work outside the African continent. In "Tricked and Trapped", ILO in partnership with Heartland Alliance International name at least 6 African countries as origin[44] for the victims interviewed in Jordan, Lebanon, and Kuwait either working, detained or living in temporary shelters awaiting deportation[45].

The abuses African migrant women domestic workers go through in the Middle East are briefly stated in these words:

> "...the domestic worker is exploited. Forced overtime, lack of rest periods and severe limits on communication and freedom of movement are all indicators of life under duress, while they are prevented from leaving by various forms of penalty

---

44 Burkina Faso, Cameroon, Ethiopia, Kenya, Madagascar and Senegal - Tricked and Trapped, Human Trafficking in the Middle East , pp41
45 Ibid

and threats, including the retention of passports, withholding of wages, and the use of psychological, physical and sexual violence..."[46]

The above excerpt against the proscribed treatment of women, strangers and workers eight centuries ago, under the Charter of Kurukan Fuga, shows that humanity has not improved in our attitudes towards these three categories of fellow humans.

Since Africa is the geographical region that is specifically addressed here, special interest was taken in what the specialists in the Office of the High Commissioner for Human Rights (OHCHR) and the International Labour Organisation (ILO) referred to as the "Zimbabwe- South Africa migration Corridor." It is nonetheless recognised that the migration of women to work or undertake other activities such as trade for economic gain, takes place between and among countries in other regions as well. Indeed at a conference in the United Nations Office, Geneva on March 17, 2014, it was the Government of Morocco which stood out as a pioneer innovator in matters of better management of immigration questions both in Africa (because Morocco sees its geographical position as particularly central in human migratory flows between 3 landmasses – Africa to the South, Europe to the North, and Asia to the East). At the same conference H.E. the Ambassador of Nigeria and representative to the United Nations Office in Geneva, pointed out that his country (Nigeria) fully understands the complicated

46 Ibid, pp42

issues of migration as Nigeria, like Morocco, is at the same time a source of transit for, and a destination, for migrants.

South Africa is today a dream destination for hundreds of thousands of migrants from other African countries. This wasn't so before the demise of the apartheid or racial discriminatory system although records show that even then, migrants would risk their basic human rights, including life itself, to go to earn a living there. Women were among those brave migrants who risked and went to work in Kwazulu Natal to earn a living: Doreen and Cindy from Zambia, and Carie K with Dr Golder N. both from Kenya (Vivian Besem A. Ojong, 2002).[47]

The great numbers of African migrant women entering South Africa today, do this because of two kinds of factors – some 'pull' while others 'push' them. The first kind – i.e. the <u>pull,</u> is within South Africa itself. The buoyant economy, the abundant availability of commodities with much demand for both unskilled and skilled labour in homes, service institutions, farms and industries including the mining industry. Also key, is the easy accessibility involving less costs or life-threatening risks such as the October 2013 Lampasas Tragedy that claimed the lives of about 500 intending migrants when the boat caught fire at sea.

The following excerpts give a good idea about the expectations of the migrants:[48]

"I left Mozambique because I lost my family and I wasn't working. My husband left me;

---

47 A study of Independent African migrant women in Kwazulu Natal (South Africa): Their lives and work experiences (Research Project Paper, November 2002)
48 Kate Lefko-Everett, Decisions to migrate, and Leaving Home and family in Voices From the Margins: Migrant Women's Experiences in Southern Africa, pp16 (The Southern African Migration Project, 2007)

he left me with kids… I left Mozambique and came here because there are no jobs. When a husband leaves you and you don't work – things were bad for me."

"It was difficult [to migrate], I wished to stay in my house… I didn't like coming here because my children are not yet grown up, they are small"

"I left my children alone. They stay by themselves, what can I do? My sister is taking care of them, she also gives them food. And when I get money here, I sent it for them, even though the money I get here is little, because when they buy mealie meal it is finished."

"My husband has got another wife, he's enjoying with that wife since 1995, and I am suffering with my children."

"Thus it can be asserted that migration to (South Africa) is an effort to improve the quality of life (since) most of the migrants are economic immigrants who have heard that the streets of South Africa are paved with gold." (Larsen 2001 in V.B.A. Ojong's research paper, pp40)[49]

The second set of factors which push women to migrate to South Africa, are inside their own countries of origin. These include the poor or sometimes even miserable living conditions, wars and other political upheavals. In many of the countries in West, Central

49 – "A study of Independent African migrant women in KwaZulu Natal (South Africa): Their lives and work experiences. (A research project submitted in fulfillment of the requirement for the Degree of M.A. in Anthropology the Faculty of Arts - Date: November 2002

and East Africa, it is restlessness arising from less than satisfactory governance – Sierra Leone, Liberia, Côte d'Ivoire; Central African Republic, the DRC, Burundi and Rwanda and the Sudan as well as South Sudan, Uganda (in the north for 20 years now) and Kenya. All those conditions have caused waves of migrants to South Africa. Where such is not the cause, the failure by national governments to effectively manage economies pushes people.

> "…many African governments face situations where over half of their country's export earnings, must go to pay the servicing of debt while the principal, the original amount borrowed remain untouched. The IMF require(d) the imposition of structural adjustment policies that included the devaluation of national currencies, reduction of the public sector spending – cutting back jobs and services. The repression that often (went with) the implementation structural adjustment policies led to people leaving their countries…"[50]

There are cases where women are pushed into migrating by a combination of economic and physical survival factors in the home country, as illustrated by the following female interviewee:

> "I lived in a village in Kenya… [in] Eastern Kenya. We were suffering there, and there was a group of men which circumcised

---

50 Taran in V.B.A. Ojong's research paper.

ladies. Then I was doing Form 4 in school, they killed people and sliced them, so I said no, I can't stay here, I will go to my brother in South Africa. I didn't finish school because of that, so my father had to sell his farm so that I could come here… [In Kenya], they broke our tribes up, they make you sell your possessions and women don't have a say in this, and the men go and spend their money with other women."[51]

The above explanation of both the pull and push factors, should enable us to discuss the central issue of abuses suffered by African women migrant workers.

Abuse mostly affects women workers who have minimum or no schooling at all, financially poor and unskilled, and/or without proper immigration paper or proper knowledge of procedures to follow. In some countries of sub-Saharan Africa, most of the female labour force is in the informal economy; for example, 97% in Benin, 95% in Chad, 85% in Guinea and 83% in Kenya. However, although the informal economy provides jobs for many women, this comes at the price of being unprotected and poorly-paid. This means that many remain beyond the reach and coverage of ILO Conventions and national labour laws[52].

It will help to examine the process of abuses in phases through which the migrant women go through from the point of entry in the recipient country (here

51 Kate Lefko-Everett, Decisions to migrate, and Leaving Home and family in Voices From the Margins: Migrant Women's Experiences in Southern Africa, pp16 (The Southern African Migration Project, 2007)

ILO-FACTS ON Women at Work (http://www.ilo.org/wcmsp5/groups/public/---dgreports/---dcomm/documents/publication/wcms_067595.pdf)

mainly South Africa): (i) The immigration processes which they must go through or, if they try to enter illegally avoiding the authorized crossing points, the ordeal they face being smuggled into the country by unknown crooks at night time through jungles and forests.

Two women interviewees described their experiences:[53]

"If you don't have the right documents you are going to go around in the bush. Then in the bush there are snakes …I was with some guys waiting at Katembe and we saw people who are being eaten by crocodiles in the water. Sometimes you find a head, skeleton of a person who died a long time ago. And you find people who help people to get to South Africa – sometimes they rape you and take your money. Sometimes they shoot you if you don't want them to rape you."

And

> "There are taxis, which you have to hire, and at the border you have to jump because we are illegal. Under the fence there are boys who live in the bush who help us to cross the border. When we reach Buckbridge Border we have to go to the bush at night, not during the day, at night, then we have to go to under the fence, then we have to look for the transport when we reach the Messina border. There are guys there who can take and show you the way, and sometimes they can rape you or take

53 Ibid, pp 30.

all your belongings, they just want you to listen to all their instructions. When they want to rape you, they can kill you…"

(ii) The imperative administrative formalities to regularize their immigration status in order to become eligible to stay and work in the country. This is critical, but its fulfilment entails a risk as well. Entering illegally (i.e. often without visa or even passport) results in the immigrant concerned fearing to be found out by the authorities as expulsion or deportation is likely. This is how irregular women end up living in hiding, where the exploiters and abusers find them.

This is a phase where the abuse of vulnerable women migrants by state officials is very likely to occur unless the level of integrity and civility on the part of staff charged with handling migrants, is very high. On this, some irregular migrants from Zimbabwe had the following experiences[54]:

"The police will arrest you, but if you sleep with him, they won't. I'll tell them I'm from Zimbabwe. If they see that you're beautiful they then propose to you and you'll leave with them. If you sleep with them, they will tell you go… They check you as you approach. Even inside and taxis and from across the border they take beautiful ladies and you'll meet up with them at the police station. Then they would have had sex with the girls as a form of payment for being illegal. They will have finished with the

---
54 Ibid, pp32.

beautiful ones. You see, if a person wants to sleep with you, they don't propose to you, they won't tell you they love you, and you'll also not tell him that you love him.   H e will tell you to give him money and if you don't have, he'll pull you to the side and the next thing he'll touch you. He tells you to sleep with him and do all those things, you see even with you and I, I can see what is happening, like whatever happens at the border gates I can see, but the one thing that I see is that the police will sleep with the girl at the border gates. They will even make a girl cross to Petersburg so that they can have sex with her in their van."

And

"It was in 1993 my husband left me with two kids, he decided to go on his program, so I decided to come to South Africa. I went to Beitbridge on foot up to the river. I didn't have any money, any passport, it was through the rural areas that I walked from there to the river and it was at night, at the river we found soldiers who wanted money if we did not have money, they demanded sex. I slept with the soldiers because I didn't even have a single cent, then I crossed to the farm next to Limpopo to work there."

A Mozambican migrant woman worker also narrated a situation not very different yet given the geographical positions of Mozambique and Zimbabwe with South Africa, the crossing points must have been quite different:

"I saw something very painful on my way home...You know sad things happen in the train. When I think about it – I don't know- at the time there were police from the border gates entering. They were trying to stop the people that sell alcohol from coming inside because those people sell alcohol and send, they steal people's belongings... I saw something painful. I saw something very painful, there was this white policeman that saw a young girl, you see? These black officers were on the lookout for other people on behalf of this man. He was having sex with this girl. You see, there at the doors? These guys were on the lookout so that there won't be anyone coming in since it is the last coach. This police was having sex with this girl. If you don't have an ID, right? This person is younger than I am and you are the police officer. You are here to search people in the train; you'll stop searching people to go to see the other one you'll take her to the door... Because I don't have an ID and no passport, you'll have sex with him. What else can I do?"[55]

55 Ibid, pp32

(iii) It would be expected, then, that for those migrant women with the required papers and who appropriately fulfil immigration formalities, abuse by unscrupulous state agents is avoided. Unfortunately, available information by researchers on the lives of migrant women workers does not show this to be the case. The migrant woman's foreignness is a terrible stigma which she carries with her everywhere she goes – leading to her discrimination and exclusion by both ordinary citizens of South Africa and state agents. Literature speaks of foreign women's inescapable identification despite their pigmentation that should make then easily blend with the local womenfolk. Police or immigration staff are said to be able to tell on sight and even from a distance whether or not a woman is a migrant. According to researcher's migrant women may walk differently, dress differently, or even wear foreign perfumes. Identification for mistreatment becomes even easier when the woman speaks in response to a question asked. She will most likely respond in English instead of speaking any of the native black peoples' languages – a clear sign that she is a foreigner. Moreover, her accent will also be identified as non-South African.

Studies undertaken reveal that citizens of South Africa today, mainly fellow black South Africans, do not like, and even hate, foreigners from other African countries. This aspect which might have been limited to informal interactions between a migrant woman and a native one, unfortunately finds its way to those South Africans who hold official positions in institutions such as the Police, Immigration officials, customs staff, medical personnel like nurses, and even taxi drivers. The **xenophobia** phenomenon in South Africa has had sufficient media coverage in recent years. We should briefly reflect on this negative aspect of the South African people – which is unjustifiable but perhaps understandable.

First, we should acknowledge that migration is a worldwide phenomenon which is now being accelerated by forces of globalization. Every country in the world today is faced with economic challenges where national wellbeing must be jealously safeguarded. Developed countries of the North make the obtaining of entry visas of any kind extremely difficult. Unemployment and economic fragility lead Europe to tighten border surveillance to the extent that in some countries, irregular migrants are literally treated as undesirable "criminals"! Where is humanity?

In the second place, South Africa unlike Monaco, Great Britain or Australia, (but like the United States) is not isolated, or difficult to access by interested migrants. With a 3021-mile long porous borderline shared with Botswana, Lesotho, Mozambique, Namibia, Swaziland, and Zimbabwe, South Africa is in a particularly difficult situation to effectively control an influx of migrants. Additionally, like all other countries in its category of relative economic prosperity and political tranquillity, South Africa is a magnet for persons living in poverty, unemployment or under political suffocation at home. For these reasons, migrants from distant African countries such as Somalia, Ethiopia, Sudan, Kenya, Ivory Coast, Central African Republic, Liberia, Sierra Leone, Burundi, and the Democratic Republic of Congo, have run to South Africa in big numbers. Sadly, all these persons aren't angels.

What does this mean in practical terms for enlightened Africans – South Africans themselves - and friends (brothers and sisters) of South Africa? To plead for humane treatment of women African migrant workers in South Africa, the above elements must be clearly understood for criticism to be fair or constructive. The rest of this paper turns to this constructive responsible duty:

To be fair in doing this, we must first state some facts.

South Africa, as a democratic nation and society is relatively new – both by African and world standards. Generally, respect for human rights practices in South Africa only dates from 1994, i.e. only two decades, compared to nations such as Egypt or Ghana where exercising independent democratic government has been on since 1922 and 1957 respectively. This relative newness to established human rights norms, is illustrated, for example, by the fact that South Africa only ratified the 1947 (No.81) Labour Inspection Convention on 20 June 2013 whereas Egypt and Ghana ratified it as long ago as October 1956 and July 1959 respectively.

Added to this are the bad sequels of the dominant anti-foreign (black) people culture which prevailed in South Africa under the apartheid regime for nearly half a century from its formal institution in 1948. That the victims of that dreadful system are the black people in power today does not necessarily mean they can't treat other people in ways that are unjust. Historians record the horrible injustices, discrimination and humiliation Jewish people suffered for centuries in Western Europe – and lovers of literature will have read about or seen

William Shakespeare's play - The Merchant of Venice on '*Shylock the Jew*' which dates back to the 16th century.[56] Yet in spite of such painful history, it hasn't been possible for the world to bring peace between the Jewish state and the Palestinians, a cousin people, for now well over sixty years!

Researchers have thus documented cases where South African women harassed, humiliated, insulted and discriminated fellow black African women purely because the latter were migrants and/or in precarious social conditions. One of many testimonies by migrant women workers recorded during verbatim in Voices from the Margins: Migrant women experiences in Southern Africa reflects this.

Four interviewees narrate forms of discrimination to which they were subjected for being foreigners. Importantly, in these cases it is nurses who refused to offer kindness to needy fellow women because the patients did not speak the local South African languages. Two of the recordings are reproduced below[57]:

> "When I was pregnant, I went to the clinic
> and the nurses just said speak the South
> Africa accent. I was seven months pregnant
> and I went there not knowing only English,
> no other language, and they were saying
> this is South Africa speak our language.
> They didn't attend me and they didn't pay
> attention to me, and everyone they just

56   For a very instructive reading on Jews in Europe and England in particular during the 1th Century, see an article by Jami Rogers (http://www.pbs.org/wgbh/masterpiece/merchant/ei_shylock.html) Also, according to some other sources it is believed that The Merchant of Venice was first performed between 1596 and 1597. (http://www.william-shakespeare.info/shakespeare-play-merchant-of-venice.htm). consulted on line on March 21, 2014.

57 Kate Lefko-Everett, Decisions to migrate, and Leaving Home and family in Voices From the Margins: Migrant Women's Experiences in Southern Africa, pp 54, 55, 58 (The Southern African Migration Project, 2007)

passed by me and attending to other South Africans who were pregnant. And I went there early in the morning and I came there about two beds or something. They treated me but late, they did not pay attention to me. They came later on and say what are you saying now. It was my first time when I went to register my name at the clinic. They did attend to me well, but when I was giving birth they were very unfriendly."

"They refused to attend to me when I was in labour at the hospital. They were refusing, I was in red and the baby was coming out alone, I was crying alone, yes they left my baby alone….They didn't assist me, and after they heard the baby crying, somebody came in quickly but I had already given birth by then….It was very painful out there in the car. People from other countries treat me like we are sisters and brothers. Even in hospital they treat us bad…."

The above hardships experienced by migrant women should be seen as largely away from what the official attitude is. Another interviewee makes this statement which points in that direction:

"I think the government doesn't [have] any issues with anybody who's got their papers. Okay, as the human being outside the community, if you're a man the people are always scared of you, so if you walk around Hillbrow I always think, what if somebody grabs me and shoves me into a dark place and rapes me and things like that…. What if these men – hmmmmm, coming towards me. What if he takes my phone or rapes me or kills me for no reason…"

Migrant African women suffer serious abuses wherever they are, regardless of their countries of origin. Up till now the focus has been on Southern Africa with South Africa as the central receiving country. An African migrant woman who was interviewed in Lebanon recounts[58]:

"I arrived at 3am. Upon arrival, the border guard took my passport. I was shocked but couldn't do anything. I received no explanation but once I took my luggage, I had to follow the man in uniform, and I was thrown into a room full of girls. There were about 30 sleeping on the floor. I didn't have my passport and was very angry. I knew it was not right. I asked many times: 'Can I speak to somebody?' I talked about my rights. They told me 'Wait for your Madam to take you.' At 10 am I was still in this room, very angry. I said I wanted to talk to someone and make a call. From that moment they monitored me very closely. I was not allowed to go to the bathroom. Some of the girls had been in this room for three days. At 3pm my name was called. A man came and my passport was given

---

58 Interview with Kenyan domestic worker, Lebanon 24 September 2011, Helene Harroff-Tavel and Alix Nasri, Tricked and trapped: Human Trafficking in the Middle East. ILO in collaboration with Heartland Alliance, pp53.

directly to him. On the way out of the airport he explained that I was going to work as a domestic in family...."

The information which has been examined above clearly shows that the plight of migrant African women workers is far beyond what the victims themselves can deal with to break free from the clutches where criminal syndicates hold them. What comes out most clearly after the above reflection is that in order to check this life-threatening experience for Africa's vulnerable women immigrant workers, every one of us conscious and concerned Africans – regardless of who or where we are - must collectively embark on a three-pronged strategy: (i) Civil society vigilance and advocacy; (ii) national authorities resolute action and (iii) international surveillance and sanctions. Below is how this strategy will be effected.

Civil society vigilance and advocacy:

The victims under discussion are all ordinary individuals; daughters, wives, sisters, cousins and aunts, of someone in society. The individual victimized may not be directly related to us but is ultimately one of us. To curtail the plans of those who trick and trap innocent women, families must jealously ensure their girl children are out of harm's way. Women with the support of caring fathers of daughters, should act in unison through associations or clubs, to share information on the possible root causes of women's migration. There are many good and well-informed women in communities who can facilitate such discussions where less sophisticated participants can participate. Radio and television airtime should be devoted to this question every so often, in different languages, and at prime hours for women and all family members to listen to. An entity such as Mothers of the Earth International Foundation should, in addition to the brilliant idea of focusing attention to the plight of the unfortunate women of Africa, equip itself with the requisite technical skills in project design, execution and evaluation. With these additional capabilities the NGO starts to reach funding sources – e.g. the specialised agencies and programs of the United Nations system such as UNFPA, UNIFEM, OIM, OHCHR, ILO and UNDP. The initiatives which Mothers of the Earth International Foundation have taken in convening this conference would be looked at very favourably, if presented for help towards any of the above. But the initiative has to come from civil society. United Nations agencies are in fact looking out for credible competent national partners to carry out their country projects. Intelligent initiatives are in shortage!

National authorities' resolute action:

Government, in our experience, operates very much like a train or aeroplane. It is where the passengers want to go that it goes or flies. In like manner, when society - the population or voters of a country or state

– collectively, clearly and strongly expresses to their national authorities how they feel over an issue such as the agonies to which their womenfolk are subjected to abroad, there is a very strong probability that some action will be taken. It is true, the majority of African women migrant workers who fall victim to abuse, probably export themselves or their skills without the knowledge, approval or formal legal protection of their national governments. This is a gap which should be carefully studied. Countries such as the Philippines and Malaysia with masses of ready to export unskilled workers, have negotiated agreements with countries such as Singapore, France, Britain and several of the Middle East Arab countries, for this purpose. On the basis of past relations with France as subjects of the colonial master, some former French colonies have continued to maintain comparable arrangements under which persons, as cheap labour, are sent by sovereign African states to Europe.

Against the above, civil society organisations from African countries should start at national level to urge, explain, and in fact demand, action from governments to protect women who, for certain understandable circumstances, take the risk of going to earn a living away from home. It is unlikely that governments would disregard such pleas from the majority of citizens. It is high time that governments in Africa undertook this issue as part of the basic functions of the African Union. Historically, owing to the unequal economic levels between countries, persons have crossed borders to seek employment. A Ugandan who was a child in the 60s, will recall the presence in the country of manual labourers on sugar-cane and tea plantations - then recruited from neighbouring Rwanda and Burundi, by the Metha and Madhivani companies. Historically the Republic of South Africa, even under the apartheid regime, had workers from neighbouring states. Today, South Africa, with the general goodwill which other AU member states have towards Pretoria, would most probably readily negotiate within the framework of ILO and SADC instruments, some formal minimum terms to safeguard the rights of migrant women workers on their territory. Other countries in Africa – e.g. Morocco, Egypt, Libya, Kenya, Uganda, and Botswana – to name only a few do receive, and in a good number of cases do in fact require, foreign workers. What is needed is for governments to adapt attitudes which recognise that there will always be movements of persons for reasons of economic self-realization. To ensure that citizens in foreign lands, at least on the African continent (this includes the known island states) are treated with dignity, without extortion and molestation, or subjected to slave-like conditions. Governments often have a soft ear to NGOs whose vision and mission appear patriotic, constructive and non-polemic. The cause for the welfare of women migrant workers stands a good chance of being taken up by most national authorities. Dialogue between civil society promoters and the national authorities, will be the surest way forward.

International surveillance and sanctions:

The above two first strategies must be in place and consolidated before the third prong can be fully operationalized. It is the combined cooperation among the International Labour Office (ILO), the Office of the High Commissioner for Human Rights (OHCHR), the International Organisation on Migration (IOM), the United Nations High Commission for Refugees (UNHCR) and others not mentioned here. For those who are not familiar with the structure and functioning of the United Nations system, the natural linkage between national governments and this third set of actors may not be obvious. However the second part of the strategy (governments) goes into the first (civil society) and the international system – (UN).

The Above UN agencies deploy huge amounts of time, and human and financial resources, on the subject of human rights defence, by fighting human trafficking, requiring full protection of workers and advocating for the full implementation of existing international standards which states have ratified or acceded to. This paper is too brief to go into all the mechanisms already in place to safeguard migrant workers in all respects of their condition.

Finally, a word must be said about the importance of facilitating access to the abundantly available information by concerned persons. Women in Africa, sadly, have not had possibilities to attend school and acquire effective functional literacy. This means that unless special efforts are made, accessing the much needed information remains limited or impossible. Literacy opens the way to broadening one's knowledge about the world. There should be a deliberate effort to stimulate interest among young women, towards knowledge. Parents are in the best position to lay the foundation for this liberation of the girl-child. Compulsory and free education for all children – particularly the girls - should now become the war-cry in this fight against abuse of the African woman migrant workers of tomorrow. Budget allocations towards the education of continents young people should be deliberately generous, coupled with additional incitements, for the particularly bright girls.

This discussion constitutes a commencement of reflection on the plight of Africa's girl-child from the day of its birth to the grave. Can Africa have a higher priority than that of ensuring the security, safety development, and happiness of our mothers, whoever we are? Mother of the Earth International Foundation challenges us all as individual citizens, national governments, and ultimately the United Nations, to respond.